ESSENTIAL SKILLS: CUSTOMER SERVICE VOCABULARY BUILDING WORKBOOK

ESSENTIAL SKILLS: CUSTOMER SERVICE VOCABULARY BUILDING WORKBOOK

Jennifer Wilkins

Pathways Educational Services, Inc.

iUniverse, Inc.
Bloomington

Essential Skills: Customer Service Vocabulary Building Workbook

iUniverse books may be ordered through booksellers or by contacting:

iUniverse
1663 Liberty Drive
Bloomington, IN 47403
www.iuniverse.com
1-800-Authors (1-800-288-4677)

ISBN: 978-1-4620-3817-6 (sc)
ISBN: 978-1-4620-3818-3 (ebk)

Printed in the United States of America

iUniverse rev. date: 08/17/2011

Reviews:

Kurt Tiltack, Managing Partner & Corporate Training Specialist, Toronto, Ontario:

The Essentials Skills of Customer Service Vocabulary Building Workbook is a brilliantly crafted developmental instrument for any workplace attempting to strengthen their entry-level client care abilities. This toolkit would provide immeasurable value to those students and job-seekers new to Canada's transactional client service industry.

Jennifer has developed a tool that informs the learner and empowers the instructor with valuable teaching aids and relevant workplace activities. It is simply a wonderful training aid that is rich with learning and development takeaways.

Bob Doran, O.C.T, HBA, BA, BEd. /Secondary School Teacher, Ontario:

I have used the Essential Skills: Customer Service Vocabulary Building Workbook in the classroom and found it to be extremely relevant and useful.

Geoff Hamann, B.A., Masters of Science Education, O.C.T. / Adult Education Teacher, Ontario:

I have had the opportunity to use the Essential Skills: Customer Service Vocabulary Building Workbook. I have found the workbook to be a very helpful tool in teaching adult ESL students about important aspects of the customer service industry and how to be a successful employee.

VOCABULARY FOR CUSTOMER SERVICE

Pathways Educational Services – Jennifer Wilkins

12 Modules - 3 Reviews - 274 Words - 92 Exercises

Contents

Introduction

The Essential Skills: Customer Service Vocabulary Builder Workbook will help you to improve your vocabulary skills for customer service and daily life. It will also teach you facts you need to know to deliver excellent customer service.

The workbook contains twelve modules and three review sections. The exercises will introduce you to 274 words that are related to customer service. Each module begins with a word list and definitions to help you complete the exercises that follow. There are ninety-two exercises for you to complete.

The exercises include:

✓ Find the Meaning	✓ The Right Word	✓ Apply the Meaning
✓ Fill in the Blanks	✓ Reading Comprehension	✓ Study the Word
✓ Synonyms	✓ Antonyms	✓ Analogies
✓ Word Search	✓ Crossword	✓ Plurals

Parts of speech you will need to know

n. = **noun**: a person, place, or thing

Example: **Adam** and **Talia** run in the **park** with **Charlie**.

v. = **verb**: an action word

Example: Adam and Talia **run** in the park with Charlie.

adj. = **adjective**: words that describe a noun

Example: Adam and Talia run in the **dog** park with **little** Charlie.

adv. = **adverb**: words that describe an action

Example: Adam and Talia **always** run in the dog park with little Charlie.

Other terms you will need to know

synonym: Synonyms are words that have the same meaning.

Example 1: The word "big" means the same as the word "large."
Example 2: The word "hurt" means the same as the word "harm."

antonym: Antonyms are words that have the opposite meaning.

Example 1: The word "open" is the opposite of the word "close."
Example 2: The word "stop" is the opposite of the word "go."

analogy: An analogy is a comparison between words that have a similar meaning or a relationship.

Example 1: Hot is to boiling as cold is to freezing.
Example 2: Nickel is to five as quarter is to twenty-five.

Tools you will need: A dictionary, pen or pencil, and eraser

MODULE ONE

GET TO KNOW

YOUR CUSTOMER

VOCABULARY—Module 1

compare	v. To look for the difference(s) between two or more things; judge, evaluate, or contrast: When you are shopping for a new computer, you should *compare* the differences in price between the stores. v. To say that something is similar to or equal to something else: You cannot *compare* instant coffee to freshly ground coffee. *also n. comparison; adj. comparable; adv. comparatively*
compliment	n. A remark that states approval, admiration, or respect; praise; admiring comment; words that are kind and honest: The *compliment* he received from his boss about his cooking skills made Aldo feel very proud. v. To praise or express admiration for someone: I would like to *compliment* you on how well you handled that customer. *also adj. complimentary*
contract	n. A legal paper that explains a formal agreement between two people or groups: I signed a three-year *contract* when I bought my new cell phone. v. To make a legal agreement with someone to do work or have work done: George *contracted* a company to put a new addition on his home. v. To make or become shorter or smaller; shrink, reduce, narrow, or tighten: The metal *contracted* as it cooled. *also n. contractor; n. contraction; adj. contractual*
courteous	adj. Polite, well-mannered, or respectful: The front desk clerk at this hotel is always *courteous* and helpful. *also adv. courteously; n. courteousness*
create	v. To make something new, especially to invent something; make, craft, produce, build, or construct: Gloria loves to *create* new hairstyles. *also adj. creative; adv. creatively; n. creativity; n. creation*
customer	n. A person who buys things or services; a patron, client, shopper, buyer, or purchaser: Mrs. Crawford is one of our best *customers*.
display	n. An attractive arrangement, usually to show off products; things arranged for people to look at; a performance for people to watch: Many people stopped to look at all the beautiful flowers on *display* in front of the store. v. To arrange a group of things in a nice way so they can be seen: Joan *displayed* the new dresses in the store window.

greet	v. To welcome someone with kind words or actions; speak to, react to, or acknowledge: My job is to *greet* customers when they come into the store. *also n. greeter; n. greeting*
image	n. A picture or idea in your mind of how a person or thing looks or is: Hiring young workers gives the store a more youthful *image*. n. A picture that can be seen, e.g., in a photo, television, or mirror: Beverley spent a long time looking at her *image* in the mirror. *also n. imagery; adj. imaginable; adj. imaginary; n. imagination*
impress	v. To do something that makes someone admire or respect you: Gord is always trying to do something to *impress* the girls. *also adj. impressive; n. impression*
information	n. Knowledge gained through study, communication, research, instruction: Once I had all the *information* I needed, I purchased my new car with confidence. *also v. inform; n. informant*
knowledge	n. Understanding of or information about a subject: The salesperson's *knowledge* of flowers was very impressive. *also adj. knowledgeable*
listen	v. To pay attention to or hear something or someone: It is important for a doctor to *listen* to what a patient is saying.
loyal	adj. Faithful to a person, a cause, a product, a company, etc.; devoted, reliable, dependable, dedicated, or trustworthy: The best way to create a *loyal* customer is to listen carefully, respond to the customer's needs, and give good information. *also n. loyalty*
personal	adj. Something that is about or belongs to one person; individual, private, delicate, or special: The sales clerk let the customer use her *personal* phone to call his wife. *also v. personalize; adv. personally*
personality	n. The kind of person you are; how you think, feel, and act; character traits, behaviour, qualities, or individuality: Loretta has the right kind of *personality* for a career in customer service.

policy	n. A set of ideas, rules, or a plan that tells a group or a business how to do things; strategy, guideline, or procedure: The goal of the cell phone *policy* is to stop employees from using their cell phones when they should be working. n. A document that shows an agreement you have with an insurance company: We made changes to our life insurance *policy* last year.
positive	adj. Hopeful, confident, encouraging, or cheerful : The sales team at the new car dealership has a very *positive* attitude. adj. Certain and without doubt: Are you *positive* you saw Gary shoplifting? *also adv. positively*
product	n. Something that is made to be marketed and sold; goods, an item, stock, or merchandise: This *product* is made in Mexico and sold all over the world. *also n. production; n. productivity*
professional	adj. Showing a courteous, reliable, and businesslike attitude in the workplace; giving an appearance of expertise: The hotel offers a very *professional* environment for its business clients. adj. Connected to work that needs special training or education: As a service manager, what is your *professional* opinion about hiring staff? n. An expert; someone who has a high level of education and training and knows his/her business or job very well: You should use the services of a *professional* real estate agent when you are selling your home. *also n. profession*
relationship	n. A connection or bond between two people or things: I have a good *relationship* with my doctor. *also v. relate, n. relation*
sale	n. The dealing or exchange of goods or services for money: In Ontario, the *sale* of alcohol is illegal after 2:00 a.m. n. The selling of something for less than the usual price: The travel agency had a *sale* on flights to Greece.
satisfy	v. To please or make people happy by giving them something they want or need: It is important that we try to *satisfy* the needs of every customer. *also n. satisfaction; adj. satisfactory*

Finding the Meaning

Exercise 1a

Look at the word groups. Then look at the words to the right in columns A, B, C, and D. Circle the word that has the same meaning as the word group.

	WORD GROUPS	A	B	C	D
1.	an expert	professional	welcome	customer	create
2.	something you buy	compliment	courteous	product	display
3.	a good price	satisfy	information	welcome	sale
4.	a close bond	professional	relationship	create	image
5.	a welcoming	greeting	customer	positive	listen
6.	say something nice	product	compliment	image	create
7.	appear a certain way	image	personal	satisfy	product
8.	show items in a nice way	listen	personality	sale	display
9.	be faithful	display	professional	policy	loyal
10.	hear what is said	sale	knowledge	listen	image
11.	to invent something	personality	satisfy	create	personal
12.	make someone happy	satisfy	professional	image	listen

Improve each sentence by replacing the highlighted word(s) with a word from the vocabulary list.

1.   In the first few seconds after they arrive, you should **welcome** the **people who are shopping**.

2.   As a customer service **expert**, you should match what you say and your tone of voice with the **behaviour** of the **buyer**.

3.   Your goal is to **build a bond** with customers so they want to shop at your store again. **Building faithful** customers is rewarding for you, the store, and the customer.

4.   You must be **polite**, ask questions, and **pay attention** in order to find out the **shopper's** needs. The best way to discover **data** about the **buyer** is to ask questions that begin with *who*, *what*, *where*, *when*, *how*, or *why*. These are called open-ended questions.

5.   Eye contact, a smile, small talk, and real interest in the customer are all things that help build **connections** and **devotion**.

6.   The most important thing to remember when giving a **kind word** is that it should be honest and **encouraging**. Remember, honesty is the best **procedure**.

7.   You will **make** a helpful, confident **appearance** if you have good **facts** about the **things** that are on **show** in your store.

8.   If you have lots of energy and a very social type of **character**, you will make an excellent **deals** person.

9.   These **client** service tips will help you to **please** the **individual** needs of your **patrons**.

Apply the Meaning

Select the correct answer.

1. Which of the following is a **greeting**?

   a) warning   b) well done
   c) hello   d) wait

2. What is the opposite of rude?

   a) courage   b) compliment
   c) courteous   d) couple

3. If you are happy and friendly, you have a _____ attitude.

   a) greet   b) positive
   c) information   d) sale

4. Which of the following could be used to describe a connection between two people?

   a) sale   b) professional
   c) relationship   d) image

5. Which of the following is a **product**?

   a) a maid   b) a lawyer
   c) a customer   d) a car

6. Which of the following is a **compliment**?

   a) You have nice eyes.   b) That is a bad dog.
   c) It's another rainy day.   d) My cat is sick.

7. If customers are **satisfied**, they will:

   a) be crying when they leave the store   b) return to your store to shop
   c) tell friends to shop elsewhere   d) speak loudly to the other customers

8. What is the opposite of negative?

   a) position   b) posture
   c) positive   d) pattern

9. Where would you probably not find a **display**?

   a) a market   b) a restaurant
   c) a sandbox   d) a store

10. What might be seen as an unprofessional **image**?

    a) good manners   b) being helpful to customers
    c) arguing with co-workers   d) clean clothes

Synonyms

Synonyms are words that mean the same or almost the same thing.
Look at each group of three words below and cross off the one word that is not a synonym.

1.	compare	evaluate	common
2.	praise	complete	compliment
3.	agreement	conduct	contract
4.	courteous	polite	political
5.	create	make	break
6.	partner	customer	patron
7.	show	display	discipline
8.	image	guest	picture
9.	amaze	impress	present
10.	informal	information	data
11.	knowledge	listen	facts
12.	listen	careful	hear
13.	loyal	faithful	leader
14.	public	private	personal
15.	personality	chosen	character
16.	guideline	policy	position
17.	policy	cheerful	positive
18.	product	graceful	goods
19.	professional	expert	protect
20.	current	connection	relationship
21.	deal	sail	sale
22.	personal	satisfy	please
23.	greet	welcome	great

Study the Words

Words that make the "shun" sound

We can make new words by adding a suffix. A suffix is an ending that is added to a base or root word to form a new word. For example: educate + tion = education

There are many different ways to make the sound "shun" in the English language. The most common "shun" suffixes are -tion and -sion.

Here are some words from the vocabulary list. Notice that sometimes the base word changes when you add a suffix, e.g., create + ion = creation

1.   create + ion = creation

2.   contract + ion = contraction

3.   impress + ion = impression

4.   inform + at ion = information

5.   product + ion = production

6.   relate + ion = relation

7.   satisfy + action = satisfaction

8.   posit + ion = position

Fill in the blanks below using the words **creation, contraction, impression, information, production, relation, satisfaction, and position.**

1.   They have stopped _____ on the new cars because there is a problem with one of the parts.

2.   The store is starting a job _____ program for students.

3.   The customer was asking for _____ about the bookstore that's opening next door.

4.   The sales associate made a very good _____ on the customer.

5.   Do you think the new policy has any _____ to the robbery last week?

6.   Emily says that the cramps in her stomach are caused by muscle _____(s).

7.   I think I'm going to enjoy my new _____ as sales manager.

8.   I get a lot of _____ from helping customers find what they need.

Fill in the Blanks: Greeting Customers   **Exercise 1f**

Fill in the blanks using the words from the word bank.

WORD BANK				
customer	knowledge	display	positive	courteous
sales	products	impression	listen	loyal
create	professional	relationship	greeting	personally

When greeting a _____, you have about five seconds to make a good first _____. Here are some tips for you to use when _____ customers:

1. Have a _____ attitude. Keep your conversation cheerful, yet _____. Keeping a positive attitude while doing business is a great way to _____ a _____ business _____.

2. When you meet a customer for the first time you should make eye contact, have a smile on your face, and be ready to _____ to what he or she has to say. When speaking with a customer, you should always be _____. The look on your face should tell them that you understand their needs and you are there to help.

3. If you know a customer's name, use it. Using someone's name puts them at ease and helps them feel that you care about them _____ and professionally.

4. You should take customers to the items they want instead of just pointing the way.

5. Once you have a good idea of what a customer needs, ask how he or she wants you to help them. A customer looks to you for help when buying _____ from your company. Make sure you have good _____ of the products and services that your company provides. Never say "I don't know." Instead, tell the customer "I can find out for you."

6. Even if the customer has said that she doesn'tt need any help, make sure someone is close by when the customer is ready to try or buy a product that is on _____.

7. Remember to tell the customer about any upcoming _____.

Thank you

Dear Store Manager:

I bought a new cell phone at your store today. I am writing to **compliment** you on the **professional image** of your store and the excellent service I received. I had a very **positive** experience. From the moment I walked into your store, I was impressed by the interactive **displays**, the large selection of **products,** and the **courteous** manner of Tom, your assistant sales manager. Although he was finishing a sale with another **customer** when I first walked in, Tom let me know that he would be with me in a moment. He made me feel very **welcome** in the store. When he asked how he could help me, I explained that I was interested in **comparing** your best-selling cell phones with a cell phone that is only sold by the Orange Company. Tom took me over to the cell-phone **display**. He asked me questions, **listened** carefully to my needs, and provided good **information** about the products in your store. He was very **knowledgeable** about the **products** on **display**. He explained the different cell-phone plans and showed me how to work some of the newer phones. Once I decided which cell phone and monthly service plan I wanted, Tom talked to me about the cell-phone contract and explained the store's service and return **policies**. The phone I chose was even on **sale**, which made me even happier with my purchase. You can count me as one of your many **loyal** customers.

Sincerely,

A Very **Satisfied** Customer

Comprehension Questions

Answer each question using a complete sentence.

1. What did the customer buy at the store today?

   _____

   _____

2. What impressed the customer?

   _____

   _____

3. What was Tom doing when the customer came into the store?

   _____

   _____

4. What made the customer even happier about his purchase?

   _____

   _____

5. How did Tom find out what kind of cell phone the customer needed?

   _____

   _____

6. If your store doesn't have the product that the customer is looking for, what would you do?

   _____

   _____

7. What is Tom's job title?

   _____

   _____

8. Tom asked the customer open-ended questions so he could discover the customer's needs and help to find the best cell phone for that customer. Open-ended questions begin with who, what, where, when, how, or why. Write an open-ended question that Tom could use to help discover his customer's needs.

   _____

   _____

MODULE TWO

MEETING YOUR
CUSTOMERS' NEEDS

VOCABULARY—Module 2

accessible	adj. Easy to see, use, reach, get to, communicate with, or understand: They built an *accessible* washroom near the food court. *also n. access; v. access; n. accessibility*
accommodate	v. To find ways to help, be of service, or give people something they need: You should *accommodate* the needs of your customers. v. Find a place for someone to stay or live; provide space to store or keep something: There isn't enough space to *accommodate* the new students. *also n. accommodation; adj. accommodating*
admission	n. Permission to enter a place; money that you pay to enter a place; admittance, entrance, access, permission, ticket, pass, or permit: *Admission* to the show was free for children under the age of six. n. Agreement that something is true, often made against your will: When she didn't answer, we knew it was an *admission* of guilt. *also v. admit; n. admittance; adv. admittedly*
appropriate	adj. Suitable, proper, or correct for the occasion or situation: You should wear clothing that is *appropriate* for your workplace. *also adv. appropriately, n. appropriateness*
atmosphere	n. The mood or feeling of a place or situation: The *atmosphere* at her family's restaurant is very friendly. n. The air that you breathe; the mixture of gases around the earth: The *atmosphere* in their store is always fresh and clean.
communicate	v. To share information or feelings in a way that can be understood, i.e. talking, writing, or body movements: When speaking with a customer who is hearing impaired, you should ask that person how he or she would like to *communicate*. *also n. communicator; n. communication*
complimentary	adj. Expressing something nice about someone, praising or showing admiration: Aaron often makes *complimentary* remarks to his customers. adj. Free: Our store offers *complimentary* tailoring of all our suits. *also v. compliment; n. compliment*

decision	n. A choice or judgment you make about something after thinking about different possibilities: Selecting which shoes to wear was the hardest *decision* I had to make today. *also v. decide*
disability	n. An injury or illness that makes it hard for someone to do things that other people do, e.g., being blind, deaf, or unable to walk: When helping any customer with a *disability* you should take your time, be patient, and let the customer help you understand his or her needs. *also v. disable; n. disabled*
disappoint	v. Fail to make someone happy; cause someone to feel unhappy: I'm sorry to *disappoint* you, but we are sold out of black scarves. *also n. disappointment, adj. disappointing*
estimate	v. To guess, approximate, or assess the size, cost, or value of something: They *estimate* that the delivery will take two weeks. n. A guess of what the value, size, amount, or cost of something might be: The *estimate* from the plumber was higher than I expected. *also n. estimation*
experience	n. Knowledge or understanding gained from seeing or doing something: The best way to learn is through *experience*. Rebecca does not have enough *experience* for the job. n. Something that happens to you that has an effect on how you feel: The customer told me she had a terrific shopping *experience* here. v. to meet with, undergo, or feel something: You may *experience* a little nausea when the plane first takes off. *also adj. experiential*
facility	n. A building or place where an activity happens; a service or resource: They are building a large athletic *facility* along that road.
feedback	n. An opinion, advice, criticism, comment, reaction, or response about something: We had excellent *feedback* from the customers about our new services. n. A sudden, loud, high, unpleasant noise that sometimes comes from electronics like amplifiers or microphones: The *feedback* from the microphone was very loud.
increase	v. To make something bigger in amount or size; rise, grow, step up, enlarge, enhance, add to, raise, amplify, or boost something: The owners told us they will *increase* our pay next month.

	n. A rise, growth, escalation, spread, or expansion in the amount or size of something: The manager ordered an *increase* in production.
influence	v. To affect or change the way that someone sees, thinks, or feels about something; to affect a decision: Samantha will *influence* Mark's decision about where they spend Christmas next year. n. The power to have an effect on people or things: My older sister has had a big *influence* on where I shop and what I buy. *also adj. influential*
organization	n. A group of people who work together to get something done or make something happen; a business, company, corporation, group, establishment, or club: Alan works for a local health *organization*. n. The planning of an event or activity; order or neatness: Helen helped with the *organization* of her parents' fiftieth wedding anniversary. *also adj. organizational*
recommend	v. To suggest that something should be done; to tell someone that a product, service, or person is very good or better than all others: I would *recommend* these tires for your car because they are the best. *also n. recommendation*
resources	n. People, products, or services that are useful or valuable: The manager created a map to help guests find *resources* that are close to the hotel, such as shopping, restaurants, and theatres. *also adj. resourceful*
sales associate	n. A person whose job is to show, explain, and sell products or services: Hans works as a *sales associate* at an electronics store.
sense	n. Intelligence, brains, wisdom, common sense, logic, or good judgment: The little boy had the *sense* not to play on the busy road. n. The way a person takes in information about the physical world, e.g., sight, taste, or smell: I have a terrific *sense* of smell. v. Have a feeling, impression, or sensation: I *sense* that you're a little angry. v. To feel or experience something without being able to explain how: The police officer *sensed* what was about to happen. *also n. sensation; adj. sensational; adj. sensible*

train	v. Prepare for a job, activity, or sport; learn skills by thinking or doing; teach, coach, educate, instruct, guide, prepare, tutor, or school a person or group: I had to *train* the new employee how to answer the phones and use the computer. n. A vehicle that runs on tracks and carries people or products: Many products are transported across Canada by *train*.
unique	adj. Being the only one, one of a kind, unusual, or special in some way: Everyone has a *unique* fingerprint.

Finding the Meaning

Look at the word groups. Then look at the words to the right in columns A, B, C, and D. Circle the word that has the same meaning as the word group.

	WORD GROUPS	A	B	C	D
1.	someone who sells things	unique	resources	sales associate	disappoint
2.	useful information	recommend	resources	atmosphere	appropriate
3.	to affect the way you think about something	complimentary	unique	communicate	influence
4.	you can do this with sign language	communicate	atmosphere	disappoint	disabilities
5.	find ways to help	accommodate	atmosphere	appropriate	disappoint
6.	to say something is the best	communicate	recommend	disappoint	unique
7.	one of a kind	unique	disabilities	atmosphere	resources
8.	the right way	complimentary	appropriate	disabilities	resources
9.	knowledge gained from doing something	resources	experience	recommend	decision
10.	the feel or mood of a place	atmosphere	appropriate	communicate	unique

The Right Word

Improve each sentence by replacing the highlighted word(s) with a word from the vocabulary list.

1. A **person selling things** can **affect** your **choice** to return to that store by making the shopping **moment** enjoyable.

2. One way to **find ways to help** customers may be to put the small packages they have into one large shopping bag.

3. Personalized service could include sharing your knowledge of **useful information about places or things** in and near your store.

4. Excellent customer service includes paying attention to each customer's **one-of-a-kind** needs and interests.

5. When you work in retail, your job is to **assist with** the needs of people with **impairments** so that they have a positive shopping **occasion**.

6. If you are working alone, serving a customer, and the phone rings, it is **the right thing to do** to excuse yourself courteously from your in-store customer and to answer the phone.

7. Providing **easy-to-get-to** customer service means that anyone who deals with the public must be **taught** to provide their goods and services in ways that are **available** to people with disabilities.

8. **Businesses** that charge **a fee** for the use of their **services** will often allow support workers to go with their clients at no charge.

9. They used the **advice** from customers to help **boost** sales by an **assessed** 25%.

Apply the Meaning

Select the correct answer.

1. Some hotels offer **complimentary** breakfasts. This means that you have to pay:

   a) for drinks only
   b) for what you eat
   c) with compliments
   d) nothing

2. What type of disability would you most likely **accommodate** by reading the bill to the customer?

   a) someone in a wheelchair
   b) vision impaired
   c) hearing impaired
   d) none

3. Which of the following would be a **unique experience** for most people?

   a) checking their e-mail
   b) driving a car
   c) winning the lottery
   d) reading a book

4. Visual impairment, mobility impairment, and hearing impairment are examples of:

   a) senses
   b) resources
   c) accommodates
   d) disabilities

5. When a sales assistant tells you where a good restaurant is in the area or gives you the name of a good repair shop in the area, that person is showing that he or she is familiar with local:

   a) resorts
   b) records
   c) resources
   d) restrooms

6. A good **sales associate** will:

   a) influence a shopper's decision to return to a store
   b) provide an enjoyable atmosphere and shopping experience
   c) accommodate the needs of everyone who comes into their store
   d) a, b, and c

7. A florist shop that keeps a small notepad and pen available by the cash register for customers who are deaf to write notes is providing:

   a) customer service
   b) accessible customer service
   c) disability customer service
   d) mobility customer service

8. If customers find their experience in your store **disappointing**, they will probably:

   a) recommend you to their friends
   b) accommodate you
   c) not come back
   d) come back

9. A word that means the same as **recommend** is:

   a) recall
   b) suggest
   c) speak
   d) detest

A prefix is a letter or group of letters placed at the beginning of a word to give it new meaning. The prefix "in" means "not" or "without" and can give a word the opposite meaning.

		Meaning
1.	in + experienced = inexperienced	not experienced
2.	in + ability = inability	without ability
3.	in + decision = indecision	without a decision
4.	in + appropriate = inappropriate	not appropriate
5.	in + accessible = inaccessible	not accessible

Fill in the blanks below using **inexperience, inability, indecision, inappropriate,** or **inaccessible**.

1. His youthful _____, his quick wit, and his easy smile were all a part of Gary's natural charm.

2. Colin was fired from his job because his language was _____ for the workplace.

3. The business is _____ by public transportation, so you must have your own vehicle.

4. After much _____, I decided to take the next few days off work.

5. Elizabeth's _____ to keep a job for more than three months was becoming a problem.

Synonyms

Exercise 2e

Synonyms are words that have the same meaning.
Antonyms are words that have the opposite meaning.
Look at each pair of words and decide if they are synonyms or antonyms.

	Words		Synonym	Antonym
1.	accessible	inaccessible	☐	☐
2.	accommodate	assist	☐	☐
3.	admission	ticket	☐	☐
4.	appropriate	wrong	☐	☐
5.	atmosphere	feeling	☐	☐
6.	communicate	talk	☐	☐
7.	complimentary	free	☐	☐
8.	decision	choice	☐	☐
9.	disability	capability	☐	☐
10.	disappoint	satisfy	☐	☐
11.	estimate	guess	☐	☐
12.	experience	skill	☐	☐
13.	supply	resource	☐	☐
14.	feedback	opinion	☐	☐
15.	increase	decrease	☐	☐
16.	influence	persuade	☐	☐
17.	organization	business	☐	☐
18.	personalize	publicize	☐	☐
19.	recommend	oppose	☐	☐
20.	resources	services	☐	☐
21.	sales associate	sales person	☐	☐
22.	sense	feeling	☐	☐
23.	train	teach	☐	☐
24.	unique	ordinary	☐	☐

Fill in the Blanks

Fill in the blanks using the words from the word bank.

WORD BANK				
atmosphere	appropriately	admission	accessible	trained
estimate	facility	feedback	facility	recommend
accommodated	sales associate	experience	complimentary	disabilities

We are asking staff to suggest questions that could be added to the customer

_____ survey for the sports _____ and gift shop. Please add

your suggestions to this list. Your help is appreciated.

1. How attentive and understanding was the _____ to your needs?

2. Were all the products and services _____, especially for people

    with _____?

3. Were all of your needs _____?

4. Did you find the _____ fees reasonable?

5. Was the sales associate properly _____ and knowledgeable about

    the products and services in the gift shop?

6. Was the sales associate dressed _____?

7. Were you offered _____ product samples, coupons, discounts, or

    other promotions?

8. Was the setup of the gift shop visually appealing?

9. Was the _____ pleasant?

10. How long would you _____ you were in the store?

11. If you returned an item, did you understand our return policy prior to your return?

12. Would you _____ this store to friends and family?

13. How would you rate your overall _____?

14. Please provide your email address so that our _____ director or one of our

    professional staff can contact you with promotional items and a follow up to this

    survey.

Accessible Customer Service

Read the passage and then answer the questions that follow it.

Nearly 1.85 million people in Ontario have **disabilities**. That is 15.5% of Ontario's population. As people grow older, the number of people with disabilities will **increase**. It is expected that by the year 2021, the number of seniors (people over 65) with disabilities will outnumber the 25–64 year olds with disabilities. By 2025 it is expected that there will be 1.25 million seniors with disabilities in Ontario. That's why it's very important to make businesses and public places in Ontario more **accessible** to everyone who lives and visits here. Accessibility also makes good business **sense**. Customers with disabilities want a positive customer service **experience** and they have a lot of **influence**. It is **estimated** that customers with disabilities spend 25 billion dollars every year.

The Province has written a new Accessible Customer Service Standard. On January 1, 2012, any **organization** with at least one employee will have to follow the rules of the new standard. This includes all places of worship, stores, theatres, restaurants, schools, public transportation, government offices, hospitals, libraries, and recreation centres.

These organizations must:

1. Develop **appropriate** customer service policies and procedures for serving people with disabilities.

2. Have a **policy** that allows people to use their assistive devices (e.g., cane) to access goods and services.

3. **Communicate** with a person with a disability in a personalized manner that takes into account his or her disability (e.g. in writing, or with sign language when serving a customer who is deaf).

4. Allow people with disabilities to be attended by their guide dog or service animal in areas of the business that are open to the public.

5. Allow people with disabilities who rely on a support person to bring that person with them while accessing goods or services available to the general public.

6. Where **admission** fees are charged, post the fee policy that applies to a support person (e.g., **complimentary admission** to a movie theatre).

7. Let people know if **facilities**, services, or other **resources** for people with disabilities are out of order (e.g., elevator or accessible washroom).

8. Staff, volunteers, and contractors must be **trained** to **accommodate** customers with disabilities.

9. Let customers with disabilities provide **feedback** on how their needs were met, and establish a way to respond and take action on any complaints or **recommendations**.

Comprehension Questions

Answer each question using a complete sentence.

1. What is the title of the new standard?

   _____

   _____

2. How many people in Ontario have disabilities?

   _____

   _____

3. What is an assistive device?

   _____

   _____

4. How much money do people with disabilities spend every year?

   _____

   _____

5. Name one task that a support person might do to help someone with a disability.

   _____

   _____

6. When does the new standard come into effect?

   _____

   _____

7. Why is the number of people with disabilities growing?

   _____

   _____

8. Why does accessible customer service make good business sense?

   _____

   _____

Word Search:

Meeting Your Customers' Needs

```
S  S  R  E  S  O  U  R  C  E  S  R  A  B  C  D
U  N  I  Q  U  E  V  N  B  M  K  E  P  E  E  K
A  D  M  I  S  S  I  O  N  N  B  C  P  F  Y  M
A  Y  D  W  P  T  R  A  I  N  O  O  R  G  T  Y
C  N  E  G  I  I  Q  A  N  J  L  M  O  D  I  O
C  L  C  E  H  M  U  E  F  F  L  M  P  S  L  R
O  D  I  X  G  A  E  F  L  F  J  E  R  R  I  G
M  R  S  C  F  T  B  G  U  D  H  N  I  G  B  A
M  T  I  B  D  E  C  A  E  W  G  D  A  D  A  N
O  Y  O  C  O  M  M  U  N  I  C  A  T  E  S  I
D  H  N  C  U  M  N  B  C  E  R  T  E  T  I  Z
A  J  T  E  T  R  F  E  E  D  B  A  C  K  D  A
T  A  C  C  E  S  S  I  B  L  E  K  M  H  F  T
E  R  E  H  P  S  O  M  T  A  I  I  H  W  F  I
X  C  O  M  P  L  I  M  E  N  T  A  R  Y  J  O
S  C  D  G  E  C  N  E  I  R  E  P  X  E  U  N
```

ACCESSIBLE	COMPLIMENTARY	INFLUENCE
ACCOMMODATE	DECISION	ORGANIZATION
ADMISSION	DISABILITY	RECOMMEND
APPROPRIATE	ESTIMATE	RESOURCES
ATMOSPHERE	EXPERIENCE	TRAIN
COMMUNICATE	FEEDBACK	UNIQUE

MODULE THREE

BUILDING RELATIONSHIPS

VOCABULARY—Module 3

abusive	adj. Using words or actions that are violent, offensive, insulting, rude, cruel, or mean: The way she spoke to him was very *abusive*. *also n. abuse; v. abuse; n. abuser*
alternative	n. Something that is different from something else or different from the usual; an additional choice: She ate salad because the *alternative* was junk food. adj. Describes things that are thought to be different or unusual and often supported by a group of people: The restaurant offered an *alternative* menu for vegetarians. *also v. alternate; adj. alternate; adv. alternatively*
apologize	v. Say sorry, express regret, ask for forgiveness for something that has been done to cause someone problems or unhappiness: The delivery man tried to *apologize* for stepping on my package, but I was too upset to listen. *also adj. apologetic; adv. apologetically*
approach	v. To move towards, advance, come closer to, or nearer to something or someone: Chris stood outside the station watching the train *approach*. v. To deal with, tackle, handle, manage, attempt, or consider something: Miranda wasn't sure how to *approach* the problem. v. Speak to, write to, or visit someone to do something like make a request or an agreement; talk to, contact, or get in touch with: We plan to *approach* the bank about a loan. n. A way of thinking about or doing something; a method, tactic, style, or attitude: Her *approach* to handling customers is very professional. *also adj. approachable*
attitude	n. A feeling or opinion about something or someone; an approach, outlook, manner, position, thought, way of thinking, point of view, way of behaving, or standpoint: It is important to have a positive *attitude* when you work in customer service.
attract	v. To pull or draw something or someone closer; be a magnet, appeal to, fascinate, charm, interest: Magnets *attract* metal. The mall is trying to *attract* new customers to the stores. *also adj. attractive, n. attraction*

available	adj. Able to be bought, reached, or used; on hand, obtainable, or existing: The paint was *available* in a variety of colours. also n. avail; v. avail; n. availability
complaint	n. To say that something is wrong or to make a criticism, grievance, or objection: He spoke to the manager about his *complaint*. *also v. complain*
defective	adj. Not working properly; out of order, flawed, faulty, or not perfect: The car had a *defective* tire. *also n. defect*
discount	n. Money off, price cut, or reduction in price: The sales assistant offered the woman a 10% *discount* on her next purchase. v. To reduce, mark down, lower, or take off: The sales assistant offered to *discount* the price of her next purchase by 10%.
exist	v. To be, to be real, or to be present: I don't believe that ghosts *exist*. v. To live; to survive, stay alive, or live in a difficult situation: Most people cannot *exist* without water for more than a week. adj. Active; in effect at the present time: *Existing* laws do not always protect people who are bullied in the workplace. *also n. existence*
inconvenience	n. A problem that often causes a loss of time or comfort; a hassle, difficulty, or nuisance: The detour may cause you some *inconvenience*. v. To cause problems for someone: The construction detours along the highway will probably *inconvenience* you a little. *also adj. convenient; adv. conveniently*
manufacturer	n. A company that makes products in large numbers: The *manufacturer* offers free same-day delivery. *also n. manufacture; v. manufacture*
merchandise	n. Things that are bought and sold; goods, products, produce, or stock: All of their *merchandise* is designed for children. v. To help the sale of products by advertising them or by making sure that they are noticed; sell, retail, or market: Dora's Fashion Outlet will *merchandise* their winter clothing at a lower price after the holidays. *also n. merchandiser*

quality	n. How good or bad something is: The *quality* of the sheets was better than I expected. n. A feature or characteristic of something or someone: Cindy has strong leadership *qualities*. adj. Something of a high standard: The bakery sells fresh, high-*quality* products.
research	n. Try to find new information by studying a subject in detail; study, investigation, exploration, examination, or enquiry: Her *research* into new products has helped build customer sales. v. To study a subject carefully; investigate, study, explore, delve into, examine, make inquiries, seek, or look into: She likes to *research* new products so that she can answer her customers' questions. *also n. researcher*
resolve	v. Make your mind up, decide; find or work out an answer to a problem: The service manager helped to *resolve* the problem. n. Resolution, determination, willpower, drive, self-control, or self-discipline: The customer tested her *resolve*, but she remained calm. *also n. resolution*
solution	n. An answer to a problem: The only *solution* is to return the defective product for a refund. *also v. solve*
success	n. Getting the results wanted or hoped for; achievement, victory, accomplishment, triumph, winner, star, or sensation: The *success* of the new store depends on the manager and the sales team. also adj. successful; v. succeed
warranty	n. A guarantee; a written promise from a company to fix a problem with a product or service for a period of time after it has been purchased: The toaster oven came with a lifetime *warranty*.

Look at the word groups. Then look at the words to the right in columns A, B, C, and D. Circle the word that has the same meaning as the word group.

WORD GROUPS	A	B	C	D
1. the answer to a problem	resolve	solution	exist	abusive
2. make up your mind	solution	defective	resolve	alternative
3. say rude things to someone	inconvenience	available	solution	abusive
4. the value of something	warranty	quality	solution	resolve
5. achieve victory	apologize	resolve	defective	success
6. a service contract	alternative	warranty	quality	abusive
7. ask for forgiveness	manufacturer	exist	apologize	discount
8. take money off the price	discount	defective	available	approach
9. the products in a store	quality	available	solution	merchandise
10. a criticism	complaint	solution	defective	alternative
11. look into something	complaint	research	solution	merchandise

The Right Word

Improve each sentence by replacing the highlighted word(s) with a word from the vocabulary list.

1. The **service contract** is an excellent tool for a sales associate to use to reassure the customer about a product's **value**.

2. When customers return **products they have purchased**, sales associates should treat them with the same courtesy and respect shown to a customer who is making a purchase.

3. The most **victorious** sales associates have a great **outlook**. They know how to treat **active** customers and how to **move towards** new customers

4. If you work for a company whose return policy limits what you can do for the customer, you should consider **choices** such as offering a **money off** coupon or a free sample.

5. Customer **criticisms** should be welcomed because they offer an opportunity to learn about problems so improvements can be made.

6. If a customer becomes **offensive**, you should contact your manager.

7. Use some of these magic words to **draw** customers: free, new, discover, save, guaranteed, introducing, benefits, easy, happy, trustworthy, beautiful, comfortable, proud, healthy, safe, right, security, fun, and value.

8. Customer studies show that as long as a problem is **worked out** quickly and to the customer's benefit, most become very loyal customers for life.

9. **Charming** new customers is about five times more difficult (or expensive) than maintaining your **active** customers.

Select the correct answer.

1. When someone goes into a store to complain, that person is making a:

   a) compliment   b) compliant
   c) complaint   d) continent

2. Which of the following would not be an **inconvenience**?

   a) a road block   b) a snow storm
   c) a pay raise   d) a flat tire

3. Which of the following is a healthy **alternative** to junk food?

   a) an apple   b) a chocolate bar
   c) a root beer   d) chips

4. Which of the following makes products?

   a) a manufacturer   b) a manuscript
   c) a mandolin   d) a mandarin

5. Which word does not mean **quality**?

   a) excellence   b) second-rate
   c) superior   d) value

6. If a product is on hand, it means that it is:

   a) quality   b) available
   c) average   d) quaint

7. Who would you probably **approach** to help you **research** a new medicine?

   a) sales associate   b) pharmacist
   c) neighbour   d) bank teller

8. If a sale ticket says, "No Returns. No Refunds," it means the product may not have:

   a) defects   b) value
   c) quality   d) a warranty

9. A customer returns with a product that doesn't seem to work. You show him how it works. You have found a:

   a) success   b) solution
   c) complaint   d) compliment

10. If a customer says that the toaster he is returning is **defective**, it means that it is:

    a) made in Canada   b) made in China
    c) broken   d) perfect

A prefix is a letter or group of letters placed at the beginning of a word to give it new meaning. The prefix "un" means "not" and gives a word the opposite meaning.

		Meaning
1.	un + available = unavailable	not available
2.	un + resolved = unresolved	not resolved
3.	un + successful = unsuccessful	not successful
4.	un + attractive = unattractive	not attractive
5.	un + approachable = unapproachable	not approachable

Fill in the blanks below using the words **unavailable, unresolved, unsuccessful, unattractive,** and **unapproachable**.

1. The applicants who were _____ had very low scores on the language section of the test.

2. Talia had to tell her patient that the drug was _____ in Canada.

3. At the end of the meeting, many of the problems that the partners had talked about were still _____.

4. One of the sales associates that works at the bridal shop is very unfriendly and _____.

5. Although the dress looked beautiful on the model in the store window, Samantha thought it was very _____ when she tried it on.

Fill in the Blanks: Extended Warranties   Exercise 3e

Fill in the blanks using the words from the word bank.

WORD BANK				
inconvenient	warranties	manufacturer	complaint	existing
available	approached	merchandise	quality	defective
research	resolve	solution	alternative	

Have you been _____ by a retailer offering to sell you an extended warranty for a product you thought was reliable, durable, and of good _____? Make sure to do some _____ before buying an extended warranty.

What is an extended warranty?
Extended warranties are service contracts that are intended to protect you after the manufacturer's warranty expires. That means the _____, the retailer, or a third party is promising to repair a _____ product or maintain it for a certain period of time after your regular warranty runs out. Extended warranties cost extra and are sold separately from the products they apply to. Retailers that do not do in-store repairs usually sell extended warranties from a third party. This means that another company deals with your claims, which can sometimes be very _____ and very frustrating for the consumer.

Here are some things you should consider before purchasing an extended warranty:
- How long is the _____ manufacturer's warranty and what does it cover?
- How likely is the product to fail?
- As an _____, what would it cost to repair/replace the _____, yourself?

You should ask these questions before signing a contract for an extended warranty:
1. What is covered and will that be in writing?
2. Are both parts and labour covered under the warranty?
3. Is there a deductible? If so, how much is it?
4. Where are the repairs done?
5. How long will it take to _____ the problem?
6. Will a loaner be _____ to you while yours is being repaired? A loaner can be helpful for products that are used every day, like a cell phone or computer.
7. Who pays for the shipping if the product needs to be sent away for repair? If it is a large item, shipping costs can be very expensive.
8. What documents (receipt, warranty card, etc.) do you need to make a warranty claim?

Claiming your warranty:
If you need to make a claim on a warranty you have already purchased, be sure that the problem you have is covered. Take a copy of your receipt, a copy of the extended warranty, and the product to the retailer and ask for repairs. If they refuse to help, you should contact the company that covers the extended warranty. If they do not offer a _____, you should contact your provincial consumer protection office or file a _____ using the Complaint Courier, an online tool available to Canadian consumers.

Note: Retailers usually make more profit on extended warranties that they do on the actual product.
(Globe and Mail, November 27, 2009)

Building Relationships

Read the passage and then answer the questions that follow it.

Building **quality** customer relationships is the key to any **successful** business. In today's market, the **merchandise**, prices, and quality offered by many companies are often very similar. So what sets a company apart? **Research** has shown that a company's ability to **attract** and keep new customers is strongly related to the way it takes care of its **existing** customers. It's about giving the customer more than he or she expects and creating loyalty. How is this done?

First, you should have good knowledge of the products you sell. As different companies have different return policies, it is also important to know your company's return **policy**. Although the return policy should be clearly displayed in writing, an important part of customer service is to know your company's return policy and be able to explain it clearly to the customer before you complete the sale.

Whatever your company's policy, you will want to welcome the customer warmly and make the exchange or return of **merchandise** as pleasant as possible.

Second, you should know the terms of **manufacturer's warranties** on the products you sell. This way, you can help customers understand product warranties and, if necessary, help guide them through the process of a **warranty** claim.

Third, it is important that you understand that your relationship with the customer should continue even after you have rung up the sale, packaged the purchase, and expressed your sincere thanks.

The right **attitude** and **approach** to handling **complaints** will not only build customer loyalty, it will help make your job more satisfying and will improve your customer service skills.

Here are six steps to follow when handling customer complaints:

1. Make sure that you thank the customer for bringing the problem to your attention.
2. Listen carefully to make sure you understand the problem.
3. **Apologize** for any **inconvenience** the customer has experienced.
4. Ask for any extra information you may need to help **resolve** the problem.
5. Offer a **solution** to the problem.
6. Solve the problem or find someone who can.

Remember: Customers prefer to deal with people and companies who treat them well.

Comprehension Questions

Exercise 3f

Answer each question using a complete sentence.

1. How should you treat customers when they come into your store to return or exchange a product?

   _____

   _____

2. What are the six steps for handling a customer complaint?

   _____

   _____

3. What is a return policy?

   _____

   _____

4. What is customer feedback?

   _____

   _____

5. When it comes to attracting and keeping new customers, what sets a company apart from its competitors?

   _____

   _____

6. What will make your job more satisfying and improve your customer service skills?

   _____

   _____

Study the Word: Plurals

Changing a word to mean "more than one"

Rule 1:
Add an -s to make a plural of most words.

1. bar — bars
2. pen — pens
3. ball — balls

Rule 2:
For words that end in a "hissing" sound (-s, -z, -x, -ch, -sh) add an -es to the word.

1. wish — wishes
2. mix — mixes
3. watch — watches

Rule 3:
For words that end in a vowel plus -y (-ay, -ey, -iy, -oy, -uy) add an -s to the word.

1. toy — toys
2. bay — bays
3. employ — employs

Rule 4:
For words that end in a consonant plus -y, change the -y into -ie and add an -s.

1. party — parties
2. fly — flies
3. empty — empties

Rule 5:
For words that end in -is, change the -is to -es to make the plural.

1. crisis — crises
2. oasis — oases
3. analysis — analyses

Rule 6:
Some words that end in -f or -fe have plurals that end in -ves.

1. knife — knives
2. scarf — scarves
3. shelf — shelves

Based on the rules above, change the following words to their plural form.

1. alternative _____
2. complaint _____
3. discount _____
4. manufacturer _____
5. solution _____
6. warranty _____
7. defect _____
8. apology _____
9. success _____

MODULE FOUR

GIVING A LITTLE EXTRA

VOCABULARY—Module 4

addition	n. Combining numbers or amounts together; totaling, calculating, tallying, or accumulation: Our math teacher will be teaching us *addition*, subtraction, multiplication, and division this year. n. Something that has been added to something else; add on, extra, supplement, or additive: A computer expert would be a welcome *addition* to our staff. We put a new *addition* on our house last year. *also v. add; adj. additional*
appointment	n. A formal plan to meet someone at a set time and place; a meeting or scheduled time: I have an *appointment* with my manager at 9:00 a.m. tomorrow. *also v. appoint*
assist	v. To help, aid, lend a hand, give a hand, or support: The woman needed someone to *assist* her in the washroom. *also n. assistant*
challenge	n. Something needing great mental or physical effort in order to be done successfully; tests or tasks that will show your knowledge, ability or experience: It's a difficult job but I'm sure she'll rise to the *challenge*. v. An invitation to compete or take part in an activity, debate, or contest: Gloria *challenged* me to a game of chess.
confirm	v. Prove that something is true; verify, validate, or authorize that a belief or opinion is true: The stain on the sleeve *confirmed* that he had worn the shirt. v. Make something definite or certain: The pharmacist called to *confirm* that my prescription was ready. *also n. confirmation*
contact	n. Communication, connection, or dealings through speaking or writing: Have you been in *contact* with Ms. Bowers about her new stove? n. When two things touch: Baking powder bubbles when it comes into *contact* with water. n. A person who can give you useful information or introductions to help you at work or socially; a friend, connection, link, associate, or acquaintance: I spoke with my *contact* at the bank about a loan. v. To communicate with someone by phone, mail, e-mail, or in person: I *contacted* the store to find out what hours they are open on Saturday.

encourage	v. To talk or act in a way that convinces or gives someone confidence to do something; persuade, promote, or support: Before any customers leave the store, *encourage* them to come in next week for the big sale. *also n. encouragement; adj. encouraging*
enhance	v. Improve the quality, amount, or strength of something; add to, enlarge, increase, or show off: The makeup *enhanced* her eyes. *also n. enhancement*
ensure	v. Make sure that something happens; make certain or guarantee: We must *ensure* that our customers receive the best service possible.
follow-up	n. Further information, action, or investigation connected to something that happened before, to ensure everything is okay: Customer *follow-up* is an opportunity to create customer loyalty and increase sales. *also v. follow up*
interests	n. Something that keeps your attention or that you want to learn more about; a hobby, leisure activity, or pastime; things that someone likes: In your client records, you should record a customer's *interests*, purchases, and follow-up activities.
message	n. A short piece of written, recorded, or spoken information that you leave for someone when you cannot speak to them directly: When you leave a phone *message* for a customer, you should let them know whether or not it is important for them to call you back.
offer	v. Agree to give something; ask a person if he or she would like to have something or do something; to provide or supply something; tender, present, bid, propose, suggest, recommend, put forward, or submit: I was just about to *offer* them something to drink. This website *offers* a lot of free products and services. n. When someone asks you if you would like something or if you would like them to do something; proposal, suggestion, bid, proposition, bargain, agreement, compromise, deal, or submission: We're going to make an *offer* on a house that's for sale in Waterloo.
opportunity	n. A chance, occasion, or situation which makes it possible to do something; opening, break, or prospect: I had the *opportunity* to go back to school to become an electrician.
preference	n. When you like someone or something more than another person or thing; give extra help or credit to a person or a group above others; most favourite or first choice: When hiring for a full-time position, we give *preference* to people who are already working for us. *also v. prefer; adj. preferable; adv. preferably*

program	n. A plan of action for getting or completing something: The gym created a swim *program* for seniors. *also v. program; adj. programmable*
record	n. A place where information is written on paper or stored on a computer; files, or a collection of information: Their customer *records* show that Mr. Daniels prefers classical music. n. A round, flat, plastic disc on which music is recorded: Would you like to listen to my Beatles *records*? v. To keep information for the future by writing it down or storing it on a computer: Eileen's job is to *record* everything that is said in the courtroom. v. To store sounds or moving pictures using electronic equipment so that they can be heard or seen later: In her spare time, she *records* songs that she has written.
schedule	n. A list of planned activities that have a particular time and date for when they will happen or be done; calendar, timetable, agenda, or a plan: Devon uses a calendar to keep track of his work *schedule*. v. Arrange; plan something for a certain time and date: I would like to *schedule* an appointment with the new hair stylist.
select	v. To choose, pick, or decide on something: Please *select* a chocolate from the box. adj. Top-quality, first-rate, excellent, or the best kind: The box contained only the most *select* chocolates. *also n. selection*
upcoming	adj. Coming soon or happening soon: We let all of our customers know about the *upcoming* Christmas sale.
update	v. To give someone the most recent information; bring up to date, keep informed, or fill in: I *update* the customer records every day. v. To make something more modern; renew or renovate: We *updated* the store last year by painting and adding in a children's section. n. The most recent information: Jon is preparing an *update* of the mailing list.

Look at the word groups. Then look at the words to the right in columns A, B, C, and D. Circle the word that has the same meaning as the word group.

	WORD GROUPS	A	B	C	D
1.	bring records up to date	preference	challenge	update	select
2.	a time for a meeting	appointment	confirm	message	assist
3.	your first choice	preference	upcoming	confirm	challenge
4.	test of your abilities	challenge	preference	contact	records
5.	at a future date	appointment	upcoming	update	records
6.	approve a time or event	encourage	confirm	select	update
7.	make a choice	message	program	confirm	select
8.	things you like	interests	select	challenge	offer
9.	plan a time to do something	message	encourage	schedule	confirm
10.	improve	select	enhance	records	update

Improve each sentence by replacing the highlighted word(s) with a word from the vocabulary list.

1.   Keep a record of your customers' **hobbies** and **first choices** so you can give them more personalized service when they come into your store.

2.   Use your business card or the sales receipt to write down your work **calendar** so the customer can **get in touch with** you in the future.

3.   Personal shoppers must listen carefully for hints about the customer's **favourite things**.

4.   If you **plan** a personal shopping time with a customer, it would be a good idea to call the day before to **verify** the **meeting**. If the customer is not able to take the call, leave a **communication**.

5.   Research has shown that a consumer's **liking** towards a retail website is affected by ease of use, product information, entertainment, trust, and currency. **Promote** customers to give feedback and **make certain** they are satisfied with how your website works.

6.   Once a customer's purchase has been delivered, it is important to **make sure everything is okay**. This is an **opening** for you to **make sure** that the customer is satisfied with your services, and a good time to **suggest** information about **future** sales.

7.   You should keep your customer **files** up to date so that you can let them know if new products arrive that match their **things they like**.

Apply the Meaning

Select the correct answer.

1. What is something you probably would not **select**?

   a) clothing b) debt
   c) shoes d) friends

2. Which of the following is not an **upcoming** national holiday?

   a) Christmas b) Easter
   c) Your Birthday d) Canada Day

3. Which of these professional people would you probably not need to make an **appointment** with?

   a) mechanic b) doctor
   c) baker d) dentist

4. Which of these events would you put on your work **schedule**?

   a) your mom's birthday b) a hot date
   c) a shift change d) grocery shopping

5. Which customer **preference** wouldn't you add to your records if you worked at a shoe store?

   a) size b) colour
   c) style d) dessert

6. If one of your **interests** was reading, where would you be least likely to shop for a book?

   a) a garage sale b) a book store
   c) a hair salon d) a department store

7. **Additional** services means:

   a) fewer services b) more services
   c) math services d) easier services

8. For some people, working with difficult customers can be a:

   a) contact b) program
   c) message d) challenge

9. When you leave notes for people, you should check later to make sure they got the:

   a) massage b) message
   c) records d) program

10. Which of the following would probably not **encourage** a customer to shop in a store?

    a) attractive displays b) unpleasant sales assistants
    c) a clean environment d) a large selection

Study the Words

A prefix is a letter or group of letters placed at the beginning of a word to give it new meaning. The prefix "re" means "again" or "back" and gives a word new meaning.

		Meaning
1.	re + program = reprogram	program again
2.	re + confirm = reconfirm	confirm again
3.	re + schedule = reschedule	schedule again
4.	re + select = reselect	select again

Fill in the blanks below using the words **reprogram, reconfirm, reschedule** and **reselect**.

1. I called the doctor to _____ my appointment to next Friday.

2. They had to _____ my cell phone in order to fix the problem.

3. I wasn't sure so I asked them to _____ the date of their arrival.

4. The store's website wasn't working properly yesterday, so they called and asked me to go back online and _____ the items I wanted to purchase.

Fill in the Blanks: What is a Lagniappe?   Exercise 4e

Fill in the blanks using the words from the word bank.

WORD BANK				
encourage	interesting	appointments	contact	enhance
follow-up	ensuring	addition	upcoming	preference
offer	select	messages	program	challenging

Lagniappe means "a little something extra" and is a word that is commonly used in the southern United States. It is pronounced "lan-yap" and, according to the *Webster* dictionary, its first known use was in 1844. The word has an _____ history. It originates from the Incan language Quechuan. Their word *yapay* is a verb that means "to increase" or "add." It is still customary to ask for a *yapa* when buying something in Andean markets. The Spanish conquerors changed the verb to a noun, and came up with *la ñapa*, which means "a little something that is added and usually unexpected." The Creole French in Louisiana blended the Spanish with their French and came up with lagniappe. Mark Twain discovered the word lagniappe on a visit to New Orleans. In his book *Life on the Mississippi* (1883), he described how a customer would ask for lagniappe and the shop owner would _____ a little something extra to add to their purchase.

Lagniappe is still widely practiced today in Louisiana and around the world. It is a gesture of appreciation and goodwill to keep customers happy and _____ them to come back. A whole industry has been built around producing "unexpected little gifts" to promote a business or brand. These lagniappes usually have marketing _____ and _____ information attached or imprinted, _____ that the customer remembers who gave them the gift.

A lagniappe may be the _____ of a thirteenth cookie to a dozen from a baker, a complimentary appetizer or sampler from a restaurant, or pens and calendars from a print shop. It is an opportunity to _____ customer relationships. There are many opportunities for businesses to offer lagniappe to their customers. Here are a few examples:

- realtors who _____ a sale with a gift certificate to the new homeowners
- dental offices that _____ arcades and play areas to occupy children while they wait for their _____
- a hotel that gives out tickets to _____ events
- a bank that gives cash back for using their Customer Advantage _____
- a car dealer washes their customers' cars whenever they come in for service

Today's marketplace is very competitive and it can be _____ for businesses to keep up with the changing trends. Bombarded by prices and products that are basically the same, customers give _____ to vendors who appreciate their business and show it.

Remember: Little things make the difference.....but the difference is no little thing!

Dear Customer

Read the passage and then answer the questions that follow it.

Dear Customer,

We are writing to let you know about an **upcoming addition** to our services that we are sure will **enhance** your shopping experience with us. As you know, we **follow up** on each and every sale to make sure that customers are satisfied with our products and services. When we do this, we always **update** our **records** to **ensure** that all our sales assistants will have knowledge of your personal **preferences** when you come in to shop with us. We would like to take this service to the next level by **offering** you the **opportunity** to **schedule** the services of a personal shopper to assist you on your next visit. In the coming weeks, we will be **contacting** customers to set up **appointments**. If you are not home when we call, we will leave a voice **message** or **contact** you by e-mail. If you would like to set up an **appointment** sooner, please call us. Your personal shopper will **contact** you the day before to **confirm** your **appointment**. We **encourage** you to try this new service. Our Personal Shopper **Program** is a complimentary service that we are offering to our valued customers. One of our excellent sales assistants will use their knowledge of your personal **interests** and **preferences** to help you **select** the items you want. That same personal shopper will ring up your sale and **follow up** later with a phone call to **ensure** that you are satisfied with your shopping experience. We look forward to seeing you!

Yours Truly,

Layla Wilkins, Sales Manager
Select Fashions

Comprehension Questions

Exercise 4f

Answer each question using a complete sentence.

1. What would make the letter more personal?

    _____

    _____

2. How is the store **enhancing** its services?

    _____

    _____

3. How much does the new service cost?

    _____

    _____

4. The store will be contacting customers about the new service. What will they do if you are not home to take the call?

    _____

    _____

5. How do the sales associates know what a customer likes?

    _____

    _____

6. How will you be **contacted** to **ensure** that you are satisfied with your shopping experience?

    _____

    _____

7. What should you do if you want to try this service right away?

    _____

    _____

8. Why does the store do a **follow-up**?

    _____

    _____

Review 1: Analogies
Modules 1–4

Analogies: Analogies are links between words. You are looking for a relationship between the words. There is something similar or comparable about the words.

For example: grass is to green as sky is to blue

Directions: Complete each analogy by writing the correct word in the blank line.

Word Bank				
complimentary	personal	loyal	influence	apologize
abusive	customer	courteous	defective	feedback
alternative	disappointing	communicate	listen	unique

1.   Negative is to positive as rude is to _____

2.   Fantasy is to reality as pleasing is to _____

3.   Cheap is to inexpensive as free is to _____

4.   Doctor is to patient as sales associate is to _____

5.   Win is to succeed as persuade is to _____

6.   Think is to reflect as speak is to _____

7.   Backward is to forward as traditional is to _____

8.   Open is to close and public is to _____

9.   Thank you is to courteous as sorry is to _____

10.   Feel is to touch as hear is to _____

11.   Friendly is to kind as offensive is to _____

12.   Cold is to common as fingerprint is to _____

13.   Coupon is to discount as survey is to _____

14.   New is to perfect as broken is to _____

15.   Cat is to independent as dog is to _____

Review 1: Complete the Sentence   Exercise 1b

Modules 1–4

Directions: Put a check mark beside <u>all</u> the words or groups of words that can be used to make a complete sentence.

1. The waitress who served us was very _____.

    ☐ relationship   ☐ inconvenience
    ☐ courteous   ☐ professional

2. The sales associate offered me a _____.

    ☐ listen to my complaint   ☐ solution to my problem
    ☐ compliment on my hair   ☐ discount on my next purchase

3. There are many ways to _____.

    ☐ apologize   ☐ follow up with customers
    ☐ accommodate disabilities   ☐ preference

4. I'm busy with a customer. Could you _____?

    ☐ schedule an appointment   ☐ available at a discount
    ☐ take a message   ☐ call the manufacturer

5. The company I work for _____.

    ☐ has a very positive image   ☐ is in a relationship
    ☐ dresses appropriately   ☐ has many loyal customers

6. Call the customer and _____.

    ☐ solution to their problem   ☐ appointment for Tuesday
    ☐ upcoming sale   ☐ explain our return policy

7. The sales associate called the manufacturer and _____.

    ☐ complaint about the product   ☐ offered some positive feedback
    ☐ new display policy   ☐ welcome to our store

8. When would you like to _____?

    ☐ give them our decision   ☐ records away
    ☐ update the return policy   ☐ two accessible washrooms

Antonyms are words that mean the opposite of each other, e.g., "hot" is the opposite of "cold."

Directions: Match the words in Column A with the words in Column B that have an opposite meaning.

	Column A	Column B
1.	listen	negative
2.	personal	rude
3.	complimentary	gentle
4.	satisfied	expensive
5.	courteous	ignore
6.	abusive	problem
7.	loyal	busy
8.	solution	public
9.	positive	disappointed
10.	defective	unfaithful
11.	unique	common
12.	available	perfect
13.	success	decrease
14.	increase	failure
15.	create	destroy

MODULE FIVE

FEATURES & BENEFITS

VOCABULARY—Module 5

affordable	adj. Not expensive, inexpensive, low-priced, or reasonable: We found an *affordable* home that is close to schools and shopping. *also v. afford*
assembly	n. The joining of parts together to create something that can be used; pieces that must be put together; constructed, or built: The treadmill we bought required *assembly*. n. A group of people meeting together in one place; meeting, congregation, get-together, or gathering: The students were required to attend the school *assembly*. *also v. assemble*
benefit	n. A helpful or good effect; a good result from doing something; a positive return; rewards, advantages, profit, help, or assistance: One of the *benefits* of massage is that it can relieve pain. v. To give or receive help from something or someone; promote, profit, do good to, or gain; an allowance, subsidy, or payment: Tyler is sure to *benefit* from the gym membership he won. *also n. beneficiary; adj. beneficial*
brand	n. The make, kind, variety, or type of product made by a company; an identifying mark or trademark: Which *brand* of shampoo do you prefer?
classic	adj. To have a high quality or standard against which other things are measured; immortal, unforgettable, lasting, ageless, abiding, or memorable: Does your store sell *classic* novels? adj. Having all of the qualities that you expect; typical, characteristic, usual, common, or traditional: This is a *classic* example of poor customer service. adj. To have a simple, traditional style which is always in fashion; timeless, stylish, elegant, or enduring: She wore a *classic* black skirt and jacket to the job interview. n. The study of ancient Roman and Greek culture, especially languages and literature; a well-known piece of writing, musical recording, or film that is of high quality and lasting value; masterpiece, standard, or model: The book *Pride and Prejudice* by Jane Austen is a *classic* in English literature. n. A piece of clothing which is always fashionable: A black skirt is a *classic* that every woman should have in her closet. *also adj. classical*

condition	n. The shape that something or someone is in; situation, state, form, order, or circumstance: The car is in good *condition* for its age. n. An arrangement that must exist before something else can happen; agreed limit, stipulation, clause, provision, requirement, term, rider, prerequisite, specification, restriction, or precondition: My mother's will says that we can live in the house on *condition* that we care for her dog. v. To train, influence, or prepare people or animals mentally so that they do or expect a particular thing without thinking about it; get use to, get ready, or shape up: In the 1950s, women were *conditioned* to expect lower wages than men. *also adj. conditional; n. conditioning*
correct	adj. Right, not wrong, accurate, exact, truthful, acceptable, proper, approved, accepted, or as it should be: That is the *correct* answer. v. To show or tell someone that something is wrong and to make it right; fix, rectify, amend, adjust, remedy, pull up, tweak, put right, correct, or assess: Could you please *correct* the amount of this invoice. *also adv. correctly; n. correctness*
demonstrate	v. To show or make clear; show something and explain how it works; show, reveal, display, make obvious, exhibit, explain, or instruct: On Saturday, Gillian will set up a display to *demonstrate* how the new products work. v. To express or show that you have a particular quality, ability, or feeling; prove, validate, establish, reveal, make evident, or make plain: Eileen was able to *demonstrate* that she had the skills to do the job. v. Make a public expression that you are not happy about something; march, protest, rally, lobby, support, or parade: Thousands of people gathered to *demonstrate* against the new tax increase. *also n. demonstration; n. demonstrator*
dimensions	n. A measurement of something in a particular direction, i.e., its length, height, or width; measurement or breadth: The *dimensions* of the furniture were perfect for the room. n. A part or feature or way of looking at something; aspect, element, facet, feature, component, or factor: There are many *dimensions* to being successful in retail sales. *also suffix -dimensional*
famous	adj. Well-known, recognized, familiar to many people, renowned, famed, celebrated, prominent, illustrious, or legendary: Albert Einstein is a *famous* scientist. *also adv. famously*

features	n. An important part of something; trait, quality, characteristic, or attribute: This cell phone has many new *features*, including e-mail access and one-touch dialing. n. A part of someone's face that you notice when you look at them: Jon's eyes are his best *feature*. n. Articles in a newspaper or magazine that give attention to a particular subject: The Saturday paper had a two-page *feature* on local businesses. n. A film that is usually ninety minutes long or more: The theatre is showing three new *features* this week. v. To highlight or include someone or something as a important part: The movie *features* Johnny Depp as a pirate.
includes	v. Contains, has, consists of, is a part of, or comprises: The movie pass *includes* one admission, a large popcorn, and a medium drink.
instruct	v. To order or tell someone to do something; command, order, tell, charge, direct, or give orders to: Bob will *instruct* the new staff on the current safety regulations. v. Teach someone how to do something; teach, train, coach, tutor, drill, educate, or initiate: Helen would like to *instruct* an art class. *also n. instructor, n. instructions*
label	n. A tag or sticker that gives information about the item it is attached to, e.g., a tag on a shirt tells the size of the shirt, what material it is made of, where it was made, and how to wash it: The *label* says that the shirt is made of 100% cotton.
neutral	adj. To have no opinion; to not say or do anything that would encourage or help any groups involved in a disagreement; unbiased, impartial, nonaligned, disinterested, dispassionate, middle-of-the-road, not taking sides, or on the fence: Heather kept a *neutral* position while her friends debated over which campground they should go to on the long weekend. adj. To have features or qualities that are not easily noticed; pale, drab, light-coloured, indistinct, or indeterminate, i.e., colours like beige, ivory, taupe, gray, black, or white: Lou decorated the room in *neutral* colours. n. The position of gears in a vehicle: David put the car in *neutral*. n. To have no opinion: Kurt remained *neutral* while his staff argued about the new policy. *also v. neutralize*

objection	n. Dislike something or someone; to not agree with something that is said or done; opposition, protest, doubt, or hostility: Colin's biggest *objection* to buying the house was that the kitchen was too small. *also v. object; adj. objectionable*
option	n. To make a choice from a set of possibilities; to make a selection or show a preference; alternative, choice, decision, or opportunity: Ryan had the *option* to travel by plane or train. *also v. opt; adj. optional*
permanent	adj. Long-lasting, forever, or lifelong: Most tattoos are *permanent*. *also n. permanent; adv. permanently*
popular	adj. Well-liked or enjoyed by many people; admired, trendy, in style, or fashionable: Wine is becoming more and more *popular* in Canada. *also n. popularity*
possess	v. To own, hold, enjoy, or have something: Madeline will *possess* all of the property once she turns twenty-five. v. To take control over someone or something; take, acquire, seize, hold, have power over, occupy, take over, control, or dominate: I *possess* the knowledge required to complete the puzzle. *also adj. possessive; adj. possessed; n. possessions*
shipment	n. A large amount of goods sent together to a place; a delivery: The store received a large *shipment* of men's sweaters.
status	n. An accepted or official position; rank, standing, grade, category, condition, class, type, or level: The family was given refugee *status* when they arrived in the country. n. The amount of respect, admiration, or importance given to a person, place or thing; significance, reputation, repute, prominence, or eminence: Our union representative is more concerned with his *status* than he is about employee issues.
stock	n. A supply of something for use or sale; store, supply, or collection: The store had lots of new hats in *stock*. v. Keep, have a supply of, carry, sell, deal in, or provide: We like to *stock* hats in a wide variety of sizes and colours.
volume	n. Amount, quantity, degree, size, level, number, dimensions, or capacity: The *volume* of downtown traffic has increased this year.

Finding the Meaning

Look at the word groups. Then look at the words to the right in columns A, B, C, and D. Circle the word that has the same meaning as the word group.

	WORD GROUPS	A	B	C	D
1.	a clothing tag	label	assembly	shipment	objection
2.	well-known	brand	option	famous	features
3.	not expensive	includes	affordable	label	popular
4.	supply of items	permanent	instruct	shipment	stock
5.	made up of	includes	brand	assembly	benefit
6.	positive results	option	benefits	popular	features
7.	choice	objection	instruct	brand	option
8.	in style	stock	features	popular	benefit
9.	describes an item	features	objection	label	benefit
10.	who the product is made by	instruct	label	features	brand
11.	to give directions	features	instruct	popular	label

Improve each sentence by replacing the highlighted word(s) with a word from the vocabulary list.

1. Customers may call you for **advice** when they are working on the **building** of certain products.

2. **Long-lasting** clothing **tags** are required by law to **have** a list of the type of materials used to make the item.

3. A successful sales associate will know the main **qualities** of all the products in the store.

4. You can tell a customer what the **good points** of a product are, but the customer decides what the **rewards** of a product are for them.

5. One **quality** of this coat is that it is made of fur. The **advantage** for you is that it will keep you warm.

6. The first step in addressing a customer's **doubts** about buying something is making sure that you understand their **complaint**.

7. We usually serve customers who **enjoy** a high social **rank**. They seem to prefer **traditional** styles and **pale** colours over **reasonable** prices and **trademark** names.

8. Our company has **well-known** actors **show** the **qualities** and **good effects** of our most **admired** products. Their **presentations** include **building** tips as well as payment **choices** and shipping details. These products are often out of **supply**.

Apply the Meaning

Select the correct answer.

1. If a man is shopping for new shoes, who decides if the shoes are **affordable**?

   a) the sales associate b) the manufacturer
   c) the man d) the store owner

2. What would you most likely not find on a clothing **label**?

   a) the size b) the price
   c) made in "country name" d) washing instructions

3. If something is **popular**, it is:

   a) well-liked b) populated
   c) positive d) perfect

4. A feature tells facts about the product; a benefit sells the product (it meets the customer's needs). Which of the following is not a **feature**?

   a) made of cotton b) comfortable
   c) brand name d) on sale

5. A feature tells facts about the product; a benefit sells the product (it meets the customer's needs). Which of the following is not a **benefit**?

   a) durable b) low cost
   c) warm d) leather

6. What **objection** might a customer with a large family have when buying a vehicle?

   a) wrong colour b) too small
   c) too big d) no ashtray

7. What **option** would not likely be found on a bicycle?

   a) multi-speeds b) air conditioning
   c) hand brakes d) horn

8. If a product is out of **stock**, the store:

   a) has some in the back room b) doesn't have any
   c) has some on order d) will be getting some soon

9. When selling a product, a popular company **brand** is:

   a) a label b) a feature
   c) a benefit d) in stock

10. Which product would probably not require some **assembly**?

    a) a bed b) a toothbrush
    c) a bookcase d) a kite

Synonyms

Synonyms are words that mean the same or almost the same thing.
Look at each group of three words below and cross off the one word that is not a synonym.

1.	benefit	loss	advantage
2.	classic	typical	unique
3.	correct	wrong	right
4.	famous	prominent	unknown
5.	demonstrate	hide	show
6.	status	favourite	importance
7.	stock	supply	class
8.	volume	amount	type
9.	possess	own	powerless
10.	permanent	temporary	lasting
11.	popular	hated	admired
12.	option	optimal	choice
13.	objection	protest	approval
14.	features	qualities	benefits
15.	affordable	reasonable	expensive
16.	condition	correction	situation
17.	dimensions	style	size
18.	brand	brandy	make
19.	includes	excludes	contains
20.	neutral	prejudice	unbiased
21.	label	tag	feature
22.	instruct	teach	learn
23.	assembly	meeting	production

Fill in the Blanks

Features & Benefits of an Upside-Down Christmas Tree

Fill in the blanks using the words from the word bank.

WORD BANK				
popular	features	brands	options	include
permanent	dimensions	feature	classic	shipments
neutral	include	assemble	stock	benefit

Millions of people around the world celebrate Christmas. Although the traditions of what to eat, what to wear, what to _____ in the stockings, and how to wrap or exchange gifts is different from family to family, the Christmas tree remains a _____ part of the holiday celebration for many families.

Family traditions might include selecting a tree, stringing it with lights, and decorating it with special and meaningful decorations. Some families _____ and decorate their trees the day after Thanksgiving, while others wait until Christmas Eve to put up a real tree and decorate it with lights and family decorations.

. One tradition that is quickly becoming _____ is that of having an upside-down Christmas tree. Although it's considered a new idea for holiday decorating, this type of holiday tree actually has its origins in ancient Christian tradition. During the medieval era (1066–1485), people would hang their trees upside down to signify the Holy Trinity.

Features and Benefits

Today there are several _____ to this type of tree that private homes and retailers find beneficial. The first is that an upside down tree offers a more impressive way to display ornaments. Ornaments hang in full view and are not hidden by branches. As well, hanging a tree upside down creates more floor space. Having more room for gifts and presents is an added _____ that can be enjoyed by all!

A second _____ of having an upside-down Christmas tree is that it can help to prevent damage to ornaments and injuries to young children and pets. Hanging the tree from a ceiling bracket or light fixture helps to prevent children or pets from coming into contact with heat from the lights. Having the ornaments out of the reach of young children and pets helps to prevent injury from broken glass and loss of special family ornaments.

Available Options of An Upside-Down Christmas Tree

When choosing an upside-down tree, there are several _____ available. The trees are available in a variety of colours and _____. The colours _____ green as well as _____ colours like white, silver, yellow, and clear. The trees come in a range of sizes, from three feet to nine feet, and fit most decors. There are several different styles, including a tree that comes pre-lit and a corner design, which is perfect for small spaces. We have several styles and _____ in _____ and we receive new product _____ weekly. Make the upside-down Christmas tree a _____ part of your Christmas celebrations.

Features and Benefits

Read the passage and then answer the questions that follow it.

Why should you learn about the products and services you sell?

It is important for you to learn everything you can about the products and services you will be selling. As a sales associate, you must explain the **features** and **benefits** of the product or service and answer any questions the customer may have. Product information can be found by checking **labels** and packaging, contacting manufacturers, reading articles, looking online, attending **presentations**, and asking co-workers.

What are Features?

Every product has things about it that make it unique or different from other similar products. Product features include things such as size, colour, weight, brand and style, the type of material it's made of, the price, what it does, and how well it works. These are the facts about the product or service that make it different from any other products or services. Here is an example:

Features	Sweater A	Sweater B
Material:	dry clean only, wool	machine wash, cotton
Brand:	Harvey Hill	Oak Trail
Style/Model:	six buttons, two pockets	pullover
Colour:	black, green, red, blue	black, white
Size:	small, medium, large	xs, s, m, l, xl, xxl
Price:	$59.99	$29.99

What are Benefits?

Explaining or **demonstrating features** is only a small part of meeting your customer's needs. It is important to find out what your customer is looking for in a product so that you can help to point out the **benefits** that will interest them. The customer decides what the benefits of a product or service are to them.

Customers want products or services to:

✓ meet their everyday needs

✓ save them time, money, or effort

✓ improve their self-image or **status**

✓ **enhance** or help maintain their other **possessions**

In order to sell a product or service, you must:

✓ know the products and services you are selling

✓ be able to clearly explain the **features** and **benefits** of the products and services you are selling

✓ appreciate and be able to highlight the benefits your customer is looking for in a product or service

Matching

Match a feature with the correct benefit.

REFRIGERATOR

	Feature		Benefit
1.	$995.00	a.	no charge for repairs for five years
2.	large top-side freezer	b.	will fit in most kitchens
3.	five-year warranty	c.	affordable
4.	in-door water and ice dispenser	d.	efficient, will fit a lot of frozen goods
5.	standard size	e.	chilled water and ice readily available, open door less

1.

SWEATER

	Feature		Benefit
1.	lamb's wool	a.	reasonable cost
2.	black	b.	better fit
3.	$42.50	c.	gentle care will allow it to keep its shape and last a long time
4.	hand wash	d.	warm and comfortable
5.	available in all regular, petite, and plus sizes	e.	**classic** colour that never goes out of style

2.

Product Features and Potential Benefits

	Feature		Benefit
1.	Natural fibres: wool, cotton, silk	a.	better fit, greater comfort
2.	Man-made materials: polyester, plastic, blends	b.	goes with everything, does not stand out or get unwanted attention, low maintenance
3.	**Dimensions**: height, width, extra long, extra large, petite	c.	long-wearing, soft texture, rich colours, allow skin to breathe in clothing
4.	**Neutral** colours: beige, almond, ivory, gray, taupe	d.	durable, easy to clean and maintain, usually inexpensive
5.	**Volume**: family size, litres, kilos, grams, giant size	e.	increased capacity, greater value

3.

MODULE SIX

BUILDING THE SALE

VOCABULARY—Module 6

accomplish	v. To successfully finish or achieve something; achieve, complete, do, finish, get done, bring about, carry out, realize, pull off, or undertake: Jess did not *accomplish* the list of jobs her boss had given her. *also n. accomplishment; adj. accomplished*
advertise	v. Tell everyone about a product or service, usually for the purpose of selling it; present, market, publicize, announce, broadcast, promote, or make known: The agent plans to *advertise* that the new townhouses and single-family homes on Meadow Lane will be available for sale next month. *also n. ad; n. advertisement*
appreciate	v. To recognize or understand that something is expensive or important or meaningful; understand, realize, be aware, recognize the value of, grasp, or be conscious of: I don't think you *appreciate* how much time has gone into completing this project. v. To express thanks or show that you are grateful; be grateful for, be thankful for, be glad about, or be pleased about: We *appreciate* everything you have done for us. v. To increase in value: It is expected that our house will *appreciate* by 20% in the next two years. *also adv. appreciative; n. appreciation; adv. appreciatively*
assume	v. Accept something to be true without question or proof; take for granted, suppose, presume, presuppose, think, guess, imagine, take on, or believe: I *assume* you will be coming to the company picnic. v. To pretend to have a different name or to be someone you are not or express untrue feelings; feign, affect, fake, simulate, or put on: Ryan *assumed* a new identity when he moved to London. *also n. assumption*
clearance	n. The sale of goods at very cheap prices so that the store can make room for new products: The store is having a big *clearance* sale of their Christmas merchandise.
competitor	n. Trying to do something better than someone who is doing the same thing, e.g., a race, a sports team, a business, a rival, contestant, or challenger: Our biggest *competitor* is now offering free shipping. *also v. compete; n. competition; adj. competitive*

contest	n. A competition like a game, a race, or a challenge where one person or team tries to do better than the others in order to win a prize: I won a *contest* at my favourite store; the prize was a trip to Mexico.
	v. Struggle for control; dispute, challenge, question, oppose, or argue: Although she was treated unfairly, Terri did not *contest* the will.
coupon	n. A piece of paper which can be used to get something without paying for it or at a special lower price: I found a *coupon* online that offered 40% off the price of admission to the hockey game.
effective	adj. Successful or achieving the results you want; useful, helpful, or a good way of doing something: Katie found that the electric fan was an *effective* way to cool down the office and get rid of the paint fumes.
	also n. effect; v. effect; adv. effectively; n. effectiveness
example	n. A way of showing how something looks or is done, e.g., a model, picture, or demonstration: Give me an *example* of how you would handle an angry customer.
garment	n. A piece of clothing: That *garment* she is wearing is called a sari.
incentive	n. Something which encourages or motivates a person to do something: Bonus payments are a good *incentive* for hard workers.
mannequin	n. A large model of a person used to show clothing in a store window; a tailor's or dressmaker's dummy: The store placed six *mannequins* in the window to display their summer clothing line.
outfit	n. Clothing; a set of clothes worn for a particular occasion or activity: This is one of the *outfits* I plan to take on my holiday to Cuba.
	n. An informal group, organization, company, team, business, unit, or setup: David opened a tour guide *outfit* in Australia last year.
	v. To provide or furnish someone or something with equipment or clothes: The new store has been *outfitted* with all the latest technology.
profit	n. Money which is earned through trade or business; the money that is left after paying the costs of making and selling goods or services: Most companies don't *profit* much during the first few years of business.
	n. The advantage, goodness, or point that can be achieved by a particular action or activity: There is no *profit* to be gained from speaking poorly of a former employer.
	also adj. profitable

promotion	n. Advertising, marketing, or upgrade which helps make something more noticeable or encourages people to look at or buy something: The company had an in-store *promotion* to introduce the new laptops. n. Raised to a higher position or rank at work: Adam accepted the *promotion* to manager of store security. *also v. promote; adj. promotional; n. promoter*
rack	n. A frame or shelf which is used to hold/display things like glasses or clothing: She displayed the new hats on a *rack* near the cash register.
rebate	n. Money which is returned to you, e.g., from the government; refund, repayment, or discount: To get the $20 *rebate* on the printer, you had to mail in a form and a copy of your receipt to the manufacturer.
relate	v. To find or show the connection between two or more things; connect, link, associate, attach, concern, interact, form a relationship, hit it off, or cooperate: I cannot *relate* to the new sales manager. v. To tell a story or describe a series of events; tell, narrate, speak about, relay, transmit, communicate, share, convey, or report: I would like you to *relate* your side of the story to Layla just as you told it to me. *also n. relation; n. relative*
strategy	n. A plan to win or succeed at something; a policy that gives instructions on how to do something: The sales team's *strategy* was to create a video display so that customers could see different ways of using the product. *also adj. strategic*
suggest	v. To mention or propose an idea or possible plan for other people to think about; urge or suggest that someone do something or try something: *Suggestive* selling means to *suggest* items to customers that they might not have planned to buy. *also n. suggestion; adj. suggestive*
trend	n. Something that is in fashion; a new style, look, craze, vogue, or fad; a tendency, inclination, movement, or development: Some years the *trend* is to wear short dresses, and other years the *trend* is to wear long dresses. Their magazine writes about the newest fashion *trends*.
upgrade	v. To improve the usefulness or quality of something; give a person a more important job; improve, promote, advance, or raise: I plan to *upgrade* my computer system this month. n. a piece of software or equipment that improves the quality or usefulness of a machine or computer; improvement, promotion, advance, or raise: The *upgrade* cost over $500.

valuable	adj. Worth a lot of money; precious, expensive, costly, priceless, dear, or important: Madeline's coin collection is very *valuable*. adj. Information or advice that is helpful or important; useful, effective, constructive, beneficial, indispensable, worthwhile, worthy, significant, or advantageous: He was able to provide the security guard with *valuable* information about the thief. *also n. value; v. value; adj. invaluable*

Look at the word groups. Then look at the words to the right in columns A, B, C, and D. Circle the word that has the same meaning as the word group.

	WORD GROUPS	A	B	C	D
1.	the latest fashions	trends	clearance	strategy	coupons
2.	present a product	example	advertise	suggest	rebate
3.	works well	effective	accomplish	incentive	contest
4.	connected	advertise	effective	related	suggest
5.	a motivation	trends	incentive	clearance	strategy
6.	recommend	appreciate	profit	example	suggest
7.	a sale to reduce stock	clearance	trends	incentive	example
8.	a discount voucher	rebate	clearance	coupon	effective
9.	have money returned to you	suggest	coupons	trends	rebate
10.	a demonstration of how something will look or how it is done	assume	example	incentive	effective

Improve each sentence by replacing the highlighted word(s) with a word from the vocabulary list.

1. This past year, one of the **developments** that has become popular is self-service. Businesses like self-service because it is the most cost-**helpful** way to provide 24/7 customer support. Customers **welcome** self-service because they can find what they are looking for or complete what they are doing quickly.

2. The big store in the mall always **advertises** the latest **styles** in its front window and in the local paper.

3. Merchandise that is **presented** at a lower than usual price is called sale merchandise.

4. When stores have special events, they often include **games to win prizes** and demonstrations.

5. Sales associates should be aware of all **marketing activities** produced by their own store and keep an eye on the **marketing activities** of **the stores in town that are selling the same products**.

6. A good **model** of a marketing **plan** is to offer customers **some of their money back**, gifts, or payment options so that they will shop in your store.

7. Lay-away is a payment option that allows customers to make small payments towards the purchase of more expensive items. It is an excellent **encouragement** program for people who can't afford to pay for an item all at one time.

8. Many large North American companies **believed** they would save money by hiring overseas companies to provide customer service and support. Unfortunately, this **movement** led to terrible customer service and a loss of customers and **income**. It has cost these companies a lot of money trying to attract new customers. They now know that customer service is too **important** to be contracted out and are working to **improve** their customer support services by bringing it back in-house.

Apply the Meaning

Exercise 6c

Select the correct answer.

1. Which of the following products would you probably not **suggest** customers try at a demonstration?

   a) coffee
   b) chocolate
   c) laxatives
   d) cake

2. Which of these pairs are not **related**?

   a) planes and trains
   b) cats and dogs
   c) books and scissors
   d) hats and scarves

3. Which of the following would be the least **effective** way to promote a new kind of cereal?

   a) demonstration
   b) contests
   c) coupons
   d) flyers on car windows

4. Which of the following would you probably not put on a **mannequin**?

   a) a tattoo
   b) an outfit
   c) a garment
   d) jewellery

5. Which of the following is a **promotion** tool that can be sent to customers through newspaper ads, in-store displays, magazines, and direct mail?

   a) clearance
   b) coupons
   c) competitors
   d) suggestions

6. A good **incentive** program to offer at Christmas for people who live on a budget is:

   a) rewards card
   b) gift certificates
   c) lay-away
   d) free delivery

7. Which of the following is not a **competitor**?

   a) hockey player
   b) baseball player
   c) soccer player
   d) record player

8. Which of the following is an **example** of an additional service that might help meet a telephone customer's needs?

   a) free delivery
   b) a contest
   c) a coupon for their next purchase
   d) an invitation to a sales event

9. The best **strategy** for reducing seasonal stock (like Christmas paper) is to have a:

   a) coupon
   b) clearance sale
   c) demonstration
   d) trend

Study the Words

A prefix is a letter or group of letters placed at the beginning of a word to give it new meaning. The prefix "un" means "not" and gives a word the opposite meaning.

1.   un + appreciative = unappreciative

2.   un + assuming = unassuming

3.   un + contested = uncontested

4.   un + related = unrelated

We can make new words by adding a suffix. A suffix is an ending that is added to a base or root word to form a new word. For example: move + ment = movement

The suffix "ness" means "a state or quality of being"
The suffix "ment" means "an act of or result"

1.   effective + ness = effectiveness

2.   accomplish + ment = accomplishment

3.   advertise + ment = advertisement

Fill in the blanks below using the words **unassuming, uncontested, unrelated, unappreciative, effectiveness, accomplishment** and **advertisement**.

1.   Zjelka's greatest _____ was finishing law school.

2.   An _____ divorce can be given to couples who have been separated for one year and have no issues of property, support, or custody to be resolved.

3.   He is a quiet, _____ man who cares about his employees and treats them well.

4.   The lawyer represented the business in two _____ legal matters.

5.   They demonstrated the _____ of the new drug through a controlled study.

6.   The famous actress was _____ of the gifts she was given.

7.   The _____ included a coupon for a free haircut.

Christmas Sale Event

Read the passage and then answer the questions that follow it.

Cole's Christmas Sale Event

Save 25%
4-Speed Blender with 0.9 HP motor
$5 mail in rebate $80

Save 25%
4-Slice Toaster, Bagel, defrost,
reheat and cancel button $24

SAY HELLO TO YOUR HOLIDAY HELPERS

When your house fills with holiday guests, you may need a little extra help. Entertain with confidence using our stylish Bohtek appliances.

Save 30%
Even Heat Slow Cooker 5-quart,
removable crock. High, Low and
Warm/Simmer Switch $20

Save 30%
10-Speed Stand Mixer with
5-quart capacity, 325 watt motor
$160

Save 30%
Espresso Machine, Perfect espresso
at a touch of a button Demonstration
Nov. 26th $340

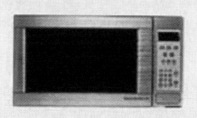

Save 25%
0.9 Cu Ft Microwave Oven 900 watts,
10 power levels, 6 pre-set cooking
menus $85

Save 25%
12-Cup Coffee Maker, Auto
shut off $29

Sale Starts November 25th Ends December 6th   See in store for more selection

True or False

	True	False
1. The name of the store that is having a sales event is Christmas.	☐	☐
2. There will be a demonstration of the espresso machine on November 26th.	☐	☐
3. The brand name of the appliances is Entertainment.	☐	☐
4. There is a $5.00 instant rebate on the 4-speed blender.	☐	☐
5. The sale starts on November 25 and ends on December 6.	☐	☐
6. After the discount, the microwave will cost $65.00.	☐	☐
7. The stand mixer has a 320-watt motor.	☐	☐
8. The coffee maker will make twelve cups of coffee.	☐	☐
9. One of the features of the slow cooker is that it has a removable crock.	☐	☐
10. You cannot make bagels in the toaster.	☐	☐
11. One of the features of the espresso machine is that it has auto shut off	☐	☐
12. If you go to the store, you will see more small appliances on sale.	☐	☐

Suggestive Selling

Suggestive selling is a powerful tool that can increase sales while providing your customers with **valuable** information. Whether they buy more or not, customers usually **appreciate** suggestive selling techniques because it makes them feel that they are important and that you are trying to provide them with useful information.

Customers expect suggestive selling. For example, if you sell a toy to a customer and you don't tell them that batteries are not included, that person may feel that you haven't done your job. Let customers know about one or two products that are **related** to the one they are buying. The extras you suggest should cost less than the item the customer has already committed to buy.

Suggestive selling can be done in person, over the phone, and even over the Internet. If a customer is looking at an on-line item or selects it to add to their cart, you can use a pop-up window to showcase products or accessories that go with it. For example, you could show the hat and scarf that match the gloves the customer is looking at. You may even use this opportunity to offer a discount if the items are purchased together. Although customers may spend more money, in the end, they are receiving a better deal. This is a great way to build customer loyalty.

Retail associates should always ask the customer if they would like to **upgrade** or add to their order. Suggestive selling is an effortless way to offer great customer service, increase **profits,** and improve a salesperson's confidence. Rather than saying, "That dress looks fabulous on you!" you could say, "I'm going to let you see how wonderful that dress will look with a hat and some other accessories. We have some really beautiful jewellery that will help to bring the whole **outfit** together. That looks perfect!" Making suggestions helps to ensure that customers see everything your store has to offer.

You can also use a **garment rack** or **mannequin** to **accomplish** suggestive selling without saying anything at all. Use a mannequin to display separate pieces of clothing that look good together so that customers **assume** that the outfit was meant to go together. Add some matching accessories to the outfit so that customers can see other products that go with the one they have already decided on.

Don't get discouraged if a customer turns down your suggestion. The key to suggestive selling is to repeat. Does it work? In the 1960s, Proctor and Gamble added the word "repeat" to the end of the directions on their shampoo label. They almost doubled their nationwide sales. So go ahead…repeat your suggestions to other customers.

Remember: If the store you work for isn't making money, the owner(s) won't be able to pay you for long!

Answer each question using a complete sentence.

1. What is **suggestive** selling?

    _____

    _____

    _____

    _____

    _____

2. Why do customers expect **suggestive** selling?

    _____

    _____

    _____

3. How can **suggestive** selling be used with online shopping?

    _____

    _____

    _____

4. How can you use **suggestive** selling without saying anything at all?

    _____

    _____

    _____

    _____

5. Why is it important for sales associates to care about whether or not they sell the store's products?

    _____

    _____

    _____

    _____

Study the Word: Plurals

Exercise 6g

Changing a word to mean more than one

Rule 1:
Add an -s to make a plural of most words.

4. bar — bars
5. pen — pens
6. ball — balls

Rule 2:
For words that end in a "hissing" sound (-s, -z, -x, -ch, -sh) add an -es to the word.

4. wish — wishes
5. mix — mixes
6. watch — watches

Rule 3:
For words that end in a vowel plus -y (-ay, -ey, -iy, -oy, -uy), add an -s to the word.

4. toy — toys
5. bay — bays
6. employ — employs

Rule 4:
For words that end in a consonant plus -y, change the -y into -ie and add an -s.

4. party — parties
5. fly — flies
6. empty — empties

Rule 5:
For words that end in -is, change the -is to -es to make the plural.

4. crisis — crises
5. oasis — oases
6. analysis — analyses

Rule 6:
Some words that end in -f or -fe have plurals that end in -ves.

4. knife — knives
5. scarf — scarves
6. shelf — shelves

Based on the rules above, change the following words to their plural form.

1. accomplishment _____
2. competitor _____
3. contest _____
4. coupon _____
5. example _____
6. strategy _____
7. trend _____
8. upgrade _____
9. rebate _____
10. promotion _____

79

MODULE SEVEN

CLOSING THE SALE

VOCABULARY—Module 7

acknowledge	v. To accept, admit, or recognize something; reply, answer, react, or respond: It's important to *acknowledge* a customer's objections to buying a product. v. Greet, wave to, or nod to: Cassandra *acknowledged* every customer who came into the store. *also n. acknowledgement*
additional	adj. Extra, bonus, other, added, or more: It is a good idea to suggest *additional* merchandise that the customer may need to go with their purchase. My boss gave me some *additional* work to do. *also v. add; n. addition*
close	v. End, finish, complete, or wrap up: He worked hard to *close* the sale. v. Change from being open to not open; shut or lock: *Close* the door. v. Block, bar, or seal off: The city plans to *close* the road for repairs. v. Discontinue, shut down, go out of business, or stop trading: They will *close* the business at the end of the month. adj. Near, handy, or local: We live *close* to a park. adj. Intimate, familiar, dear, or devoted: My brother and I are *close*. *also n. closure; n. closeness*
collect	v. To bring people or things together from different places over time; gather, assemble, accumulate, pull together, save, hoard, stockpile, have a collection, have a passion for, or obsessed with: It's Terri's job to *collect* the information from customers and enter it into the computer. v. To get control of your thoughts or feelings, especially after a surprise or shock: After the meeting, Ted needed time to *collect* his thoughts. adv. To make a telephone call that the person you are calling pays for, usually long distance: Zoe's friend called *collect* from England. *also n. collection; n. collector; n. collectable; adj. collectable; adj. collective; n. collective; adv. collectively*
comment	n. Something that you say or write that expresses your opinion: Do not make any *comments* about my hair. v. To say or explain something; make a remark or statement about someone or something: The reporter asked Pat to *comment* on the grand opening of the theatre. *also n. commentary*

credit	n. Approval, recognition, thanks, glory, acclaim, acknowledgement, tribute, or praise: Robin was very upset when her boss took *credit* for all the hard work she had done. n. A way of paying for goods or services at a later time that usually involves paying interest on the original money, e.g., with a credit card: The furniture store offered customers twelve months of interest-free *credit* on their purchases. n. Course unit: Tyler finished six *credits* towards his business degree. n. A list of people who helped to make a movie or radio program: Kathi's name was listed in the *credits* at the end of the movie. v. To pay money into a bank or store account: The department store promised to *credit* my account when I returned the toaster. v. To believe something that seems unlikely to be true; believe, accept, or trust: It is hard to *credit* that she has accomplished everything she says she has.
disclose	v. To make something known publicly or show that something was hidden: The store *disclosed* that two of their staff were fired for theft. *also n. disclosure*
discretion	n. Able to act in a way that does not cause embarrassment or attract attention; good judgment, preferences, or choices: The movie was very violent so parental *discretion* was advised. *also adj. discrete*
exception	n. Someone or something not included in a group or rule; doesn't count, or not included with the rest: With *exception* to Sundays, you can only park on our street for two hours between 9 a.m. and 6 p.m. *also preposition/conjunction except*
exchange	v. Trade with someone; give someone something and that person gives you something in return; barter, switch, swap, or substitute: I tried to *exchange* the sweater, but the store said that they were not able to make *exchanges* during Christmas and New Year's.
fraud	n. A crime where someone gets money by cheating, lying, scamming, conning, or deceiving someone else: It is *fraud* when you write someone a cheque when you know that you don't have enough money in your bank account to honour it. n. A person who deceives people by pretending to be someone or something that he or she is not: I thought Cindy was a real psychic, but it turned out that she was a *fraud*. *also adj. fraudulent*

handle	v. To pick something up and touch, finger, feel, or hold it with your hands: The sales associate told the children not to *handle* the towels. v. To manage, supervise, process, carry out, control, operate, conduct, deal with, or be in charge of: Our store *handles* most types of car repairs in our service centre. n. An informal name, nickname, or code name of a person or place; often an unusual name: John's radio *handle* is "Big John." n. A grip, knob, or switch that is made for holding, moving, or carrying something easily: The *handle* broke off the door.
indicate	v. To show, reveal, imply, hint at, or show a sign of something: Holding your head in your hands could *indicate* that you have a headache. v. Point to, show, or make clear: They put a sign up to *indicate* where the restrooms are located. *also n. indication; n. indicator; adj. indicative*
key	n. A tool for locking or unlocking a door, etc.: Tyler misplaced the *keys* to the store again. n. Any set of moving parts that you press with your fingers to produce letters, numbers, symbols, or musical notes; e.g., computer, cash register, or piano: The "Enter" *key* on my computer is stuck. n. A set of musical notes based on one note: You are singing off-*key*. v. Input, enter, type: Please *key* in the password for the safe. n. A list of symbols used in a map or book with explanations of what they mean: Check the *key* on the map to see what that symbol means. v. Solution, answer, secret, or explanation: The *key* to good health is diet and exercise. adj. Very important and having a lot of influence on other people or things; main, crucial, major, vital, or basic: He was their *key* suspect in the murder investigation. The *key* ingredient for an omelette is eggs.
limit	n. The greatest level, number, or amount of something that is allowed or possible; maximum, threshold, bounds, cutoff point, ceiling, or cap: What is your credit *limit*? v. To control something so that it does not go over a certain amount, number, or level; control, regulate, reduce, curb, ration, keep a tight rein on, or restrict: The staff were asked to *limit* the amount of time they take for breaks when the store is busy. *also adj. limited; n. limitation*

modify	v. To change something like a plan, opinion, behaviour, or law in a small way to make it better or more acceptable: We need to *modify* our return policy so that it is easier for customers to understand. *also n. modification; n. modified*
original	adj. Something that existed from the beginning or the earliest form of something; first, initial, earliest, previous, fundamental, or primary: I enjoyed the movie, but the *original* movie starring John Wayne is still my favourite. adj. Special or interesting because it is not the same as anyone or anything else; unique, innovative, novel, inventive, creative, new, unusual, or imaginative: Abhidi is a very *original* young artist. n. The first one made; something that is real or genuine; not a copy: This is an *original* sketch from the artist's personal collection. *also n. origin; adv. originally; n. originality*
prevent	v. To stop something from happening or stop someone from doing something; put off, avoid, put a stop to, or nip in the bud (idiom): The policies were created to help *prevent* fraud. The hand-washing policy was created to help *prevent* the spread of germs. *also n. prevention; adj. preventable*
refund	n. Money that is given back to you or a repayment, e.g., money returned because you are not happy with a product or service that you have bought: Kerry spent her tax *refund* on a new bike. v. To repay, return, or give someone money back: The shoe store *refunded* my money after I complained to the manager about the poor quality of the shoes. *also v. refundable*
require	v. To need or make necessary; essential or vital: Employees *require* safety glasses when they work in the lab. *also n. requirement*
review	v. Have another look at something to see if changes need to be made; re-examine, check, re-evaluate, or reconsider: The family doctor and the surgeon *reviewed* the X-rays. v. Give an opinion; appraise, evaluate, assess, look at, study or examine: Store return policies should be *reviewed* with each customer at the time of purchase. n. When you look at something again in order to make changes to it, give an opinion, or study it: The radio station did a *review* of the year's top news stories.

role	n. The position, job, task, responsibility, or function that someone or something has in a situation, employment, or relationship: One of my *roles* as a store clerk is to return unwanted items to the right place in the store.
signal	n. An action, movement, or sound that gives information; a message, a warning, or an order, e.g., a radio signal, a railway or traffic signal: A customer is giving a buying *signal* if he or she asks the sales associate to find a certain item in their size. v. To make a sign, movement, or sound which gives information or tells people what to do; hint at, indicate, show, suggest, or imply: An action that may *signal* that a customer is ready to buy is handling a product for a second or third time.
technique	n. A way of doing things that requires skill: Zoran's *technique* on the piano is remarkable.
uncertain	adj. Unsure or not knowing what to do or believe; not able to make a decision; doubtful, hesitant, undecided, or unclear: Jon is *uncertain* about taking a cruise because he is worried that he will get seasick. *also adj. certain; adv. certainly*

Look at the word groups. Then look at the words to the right in columns A, B, C, and D. Circle the word that has the same meaning as the word group.

	WORD GROUPS	A	B	C	D
1.	part of your job	role	indicate	handle	signal
2.	way of doing something	prevent	exception	technique	role
3.	show a sign of	indicate	exception	role	exchange
4.	important	require	technique	review	key
5.	deal with	additional	exception	handle	role
6.	replace	technique	exchange	uncertain	key
7.	go over	modify	refund	key	review
8.	to give a hint	signal	role	refund	exchange
9.	not sure	review	uncertain	exchange	fraud
10.	finish	review	close	indicate	signal

The Right Word

Improve each sentence by replacing the highlighted word(s) with a word from the vocabulary list.

1. Sales associates who work in department stores are most likely to play a **major** role in helping customers make a purchasing decision.

2. When a sale is **finished** it means that you and your company have succeeded and your customer has received what he wants and needs.

3. One customer **statement** that may **show** a customer is ready to buy is: "Does this come in a different colour?"

4. If a customer is **in doubt** about buying something, you may need to **gather** more information by asking different questions.

5. Telling a customer about the store's return and **switch** policy can be encouraging when a customer in **undecided**.

6. If a customer is buying a video, you might also suggest an **extra** purchase like popcorn or pop.

7. Another **statement** that may **point out** a customer is ready to buy is: "I've always wanted one of these!"

8. You must use your **judgment** when giving **money back** for defective products.

Apply the Meaning

Select the correct answer.

1. When a customer has decided to buy a product or service at your store, it is a good time to suggest **additional** products to go along with that purchase. An **additional** product you would probably not suggest to a customer who is buying new coat is:

   a) a hat
   c) a scarf
   b) mittens
   d) perfume

2. If a customer has decided to buy new shoes at your store, you could **encourage** him to also buy:

   a) batteries
   c) a warranty
   b) protection spray
   d) a toe ring

3. When a customer gives you a **signal** that she will be buying a television from you, it is a good **opportunity** for you to suggest that she also purchase:

   a) an extended warranty
   c) a computer
   b) CDs
   d) a cell phone

4. Which word is not a synonym (word with the same meaning) for the word **close**?

   a) shut
   c) begin
   b) near
   d) finish

5. Which word is not a synonym for the word **key**?

   a) answer
   c) major
   b) important
   d) hint

6. Which of the following would be a good reason to **exchange** a sweater?

   a) wrong size
   c) wrong colour
   b) wrong style
   d) all of these

7. Which reason might make a customer **uncertain** about purchasing a new car?

   a) nice colour
   c) good reviews
   b) very expensive
   d) great stereo

8. If one of the **roles** of your job is to stock shelves, your job title may be:

   a) sales associate
   c) store clerk
   b) sales clerk
   d) all of these

9. If one of your job **roles** is to operate a cash register, you probably do not work as:

   a) a cashier
   c) a sales associate
   b) a lawyer
   d) a retail clerk

Synonyms

Synonyms are words that have the same meaning.
Antonyms are words that have the opposite meaning.
Look at each pair of words and decide if they are synonyms or antonyms.

	Words		Synonym	Antonym
1.	acknowledge	recognize	☐	☐
2.	additional	extra	☐	☐
3.	close	open	☐	☐
4.	collect	gather	☐	☐
5.	comment	statement	☐	☐
6.	credit	discredit	☐	☐
7.	disclose	hide	☐	☐
8.	discretion	tact	☐	☐
9.	exception	exemption	☐	☐
10.	exchange	trade	☐	☐
11.	fraud	scam	☐	☐
12.	handle	knob	☐	☐
13.	indicate	show	☐	☐
14.	key	unimportant	☐	☐
15.	limit	control	☐	☐
16.	modify	change	☐	☐
17.	original	unoriginal	☐	☐
18.	prevent	stop	☐	☐
19.	refund	repay	☐	☐
20.	require	need	☐	☐
21.	review	check	☐	☐
22.	role	position	☐	☐
23.	signal	hint	☐	☐
24.	technique	skill	☐	☐
25.	uncertain	certain	☐	☐

Study the Words

A suffix is an ending that is added to a word to create a new word. The new words are similar in meaning to the original word, but they are different parts of speech.

The following words are formed by adding suffixes to the word **collect**.

Meaning

1. collect — v. To bring people or things together from different places over time
2. collection — n. A group of things together
3. collector — n. Someone who collects objects because they are beautiful, valuable, or interesting
   n. Someone whose job is to collect money from people
4. collectable — n. Any object which people want to collect as a hobby
   adj. Describes something that is considered to be worth collecting as a hobby
5. collective — adj. Of or shared by every member of a group of people
   n. An organization or business which is owned and controlled by the people who work in it
6. collectively — adv. As a group

Fill in the blanks below using the correct form of the word **collect**.

1. The new Employee's Association has helped to create a _____ agreement between staff and management.

2. Jin is a _____ of fine art.

3. There are many people who find _____ items at garage sales and in second-hand stores.

4. Jennifer likes to _____ Christmas ornaments.

5. Jon has acquired a large _____ of music over the years.

6. Tyler and Priya organized the books _____ by title rather than grouping them by author.

Return and Exchange Policy

Read the passage and then answer the questions that follow it.

RETURNS, REFUNDS, AND EXCHANGES

EASY RETURNS: WE ENCOURAGE YOU TO SAVE YOUR RECEIPT

AN ITEM MAY BE RETURNED FOR **EXCHANGE** OR **REFUND** UNDER THE FOLLOWING CONDITIONS:

1. Bring the item(s) to any Cole's Department Store within 90 days, in its original condition and packaging, with your receipt.
2. If you do not have the original receipt, a return will be made at the **discretion** of the Cole's supervisor on shift.
3. If a product is **defective**, the manufacturer's warranty will apply.
4. Credit to the original method of payment or a store credit will be provided as required. Some **exceptions** may apply.*
5. Your name, home address, and phone number will be required. This information is collected, used, and kept on file to help **prevent fraud**, and may only be disclosed within Cole's Department Store. Valid photo ID may be **required** to confirm this information.

*Exceptions include but are not limited to the following:
- electronics (home audio & video, personal audio & video, cameras & accessories, communications) may only be returned within 30 days
- ink cartridges, media and memory cards, books, DVDs, CDs, mattresses, and portable beds may only be returned if unopened

The following products/services are not refundable:
- tinted paint and stain products
- products cut to length or modified
- magazines
- fireworks
- clearance or final sale merchandise

Further details are available at our Customer Service desk.

Gift receipts
A store credit will be given when returning a product with a gift receipt.

Gift card purchases are final
Gift cards are not returnable and non-refundable

Shipping charges are non-refundable
We will gladly refund your original shipping cost if you are returning a gift card because of an error on our part.

If you require more information or require assistance with a return or exchange, call Customer Service at 1-888-888-8888.

Comprehension Questions

Answer each question using a complete sentence.

1. What are the four conditions for returning or exchanging a product?

   _____

   _____

   _____

2. What will happen if you don't have your receipt?

   _____

   _____

   _____

3. List three products that are exceptions to the policy. What are the conditions for refunds and exchanges on these products?

   _____

   _____

4. List three products that are not refundable.

   _____

   _____

5. What is the refund policy for shipping charges?

   _____

   _____

6. What is the refund and return policy for gift cards?

   _____

   _____

7. What personal information does the store ask you for?

   _____

   _____

Crossword: Closing the Sale

Exercise 7g

Across

2. a way of paying for something later
5. make something known that was hidden
7. say something that expresses your opinion
9. a way of doing things that requires skill
10. money that is returned to you
11. very important or vital

Down

1. to get money by cheating
2. not open
3. good judgment
4. gather together
6. trade or barter with someone
8. to change something for the better

MODULE EIGHT

COMPLETING THE
SALES TRANSACTION

VOCABULARY—Module 8

accurate	adj. Correct, exact, precise, true, truthful, perfect, or no mistakes: The inventory totals for the month were *accurate*. *also n. accuracy; adv. accurately*
authorization	n. Approval for something to happen; permission or consent to do something: You must fill out a medical *authorization* form before they will do the surgery. *also v. authorize; n. authority*
bar code	n. A series of numbers and thick and thin vertical lines of magnetic ink that are stamped onto store products. When placed under a computer scanner, these numbers and lines tell you details about an item, e.g., how much it costs, how many are in stock, or product description: There was something wrong with the *bar code*; it kept coming up on the screen as toilet paper instead of coffee. bar codes are also referred to as: UPC: universal product codes PLU: price look up
calculate	v. Work out, compute, estimate, determine, evaluate, assess, or analyze the number or amount of something by using information that you have and by adding, subtracting, multiplying, or dividing numbers: I used my calculator to *calculate* how much the stove would cost with taxes. *also n. calculation;, n. calculator*
change	n. Money that is given in coins rather than notes: The cashier gave me the wrong *change*. n. Putting on different clothes: Tell her to bring a *change* of clothes if she's staying overnight. n. When something becomes different; an alteration, variation, adjustment, or revolution: Social *change* is just around the corner. v. To replace one thing with another; become different, exchange, swap, replace, trade, alter, adjust, vary, or modify: You need to *change* your shirt and your attitude. v. To trade money for smaller currency or the same value in a different currency, e.g., *change* Canadian currency to U.S. currency: Please *change* this money to U.S. funds before we leave on holidays.

check	v. Make sure or certain that something is correct, proper, or safe by examining it: Please *check* my oil.
	v. Leave something with someone at a certain place so that person can take care of it for you for a short time: You can *check* your coat at the counter over there. You can *check* your baggage in now.
	n. An inspection of something to make sure that it is correct or the way it should be: I had to have a safety *check* done on my car.
cheque	n. A printed form that can be used instead of money to make payments from your bank account: The electronics company sent me a rebate *cheque* in the mail.
code	n. A system of letters, signs, or words that is used to create a secret message or a short form: The letters n., v., adj., adv. are used in this vocabulary list as a grammar *code* for noun, verb, adjective, and adverb.
	n. A set of rules that tells how a group of people should behave: Doctors follow a *code* of ethics.
combination	n. The blend that you get when two or more things are mixed together: I asked the cashier to change my $100 bill for a *combination* of twenties, tens, fives, toonies, loonies, and quarters.
	n. The series of numbers needed to open a lock or a safe: Only two staff members have the *combination* to the safe.
	also v. combine
commission	n. A form of payment for salespeople who are given a percentage of money based on the total amount they sell: I receive a 5% *commission* on every car I sell.
	v. To hire, appoint, contract, or authorize someone to do a special piece of work: I was *commissioned* to create an art sculpture for the city.
commit	v. To do something that is wrong or illegal; to perform, execute, carry out, perpetrate, or cause: It is wrong and illegal to *commit* murder.
	v. To give or promise your time, money, or loyalty to a particular person, plan of action, or principle; pledge, bind, oblige, require, constrain, or compel: He was not able to *commit* himself to the job.
	v. To send someone officially to a hospital or prison; entrust, give, consign, place, hand over, or assign: They will *commit* him to the psychiatric ward in the morning.
	also n. commitment

consistent	adj. Always happening or working in the same way, especially positive; act, perform, or behave: The sales at the new store have been *consistent* over the past three months. adj. In agreement with other facts or with previous behaviour: The statement from the witness was not *consistent* with the evidence. *also adv. consistently*
fragile	adj. Easily broken or damaged, delicate, or breakable: Be careful with that box! The contents are *fragile*! adj. Not strong; frail, weak, delicate, or in poor health: Although Robin is recovering from her illness, she still seems very *fragile*.
identical	adj. Exactly the same or very similar; equal, matching, alike, or duplicate: The rooms at the hotel were *identical*. *also adv. identically*
identification	n. Papers, documents, or credentials that prove that you are who you say you are, e.g., driver's licence, birth certificate, or passport: They would only accept a passport as *identification* at the border. n. When you can recognize and name someone or something: *Identification* of the bodies from the fire was difficult because so many of the victims were on vacation from other countries. *also v. identify*
outcome	n. A result, achievement, accomplishment, or effect of an act or situation: The *outcome* of the meeting was very positive.
participate	v. To take part in or be involved in an activity; contribute, partake, take part, or share: All of the staff will *participate* in the safety training. *also n. participant; n. participation*
POS terminals	n. A point-of-sale (POS) terminal is a computerized cash register. It can record and track customer orders, process credit and debit cards, connect to other systems in a network, and manage inventory: Our store just installed a new *POS terminal*.
procedure	n. A set way of doing things; a process, practice, method, or system that is the proper or accepted way of doing something : The company's policies and *procedures* for dealing with cash were very clear.

receipt	n. Proof of payment; a slip of paper that proves you have paid for a product or service: Your *receipt* is in the bag. n. A piece of paper that proves that money, goods, or information has been received: Samantha signed the invoice to prove that she was in *receipt* of the flowers.
reconcile	v. To find a way to settle or resolve differences; put right, reunite, bring together, or fix a problem: Betty was unable to *reconcile* the cash with the receipts so she had to ask for help. The counsellor helped the couple to *reconcile* their differences. *also n. reconciliation; v. reconciled*
responsibility	n. Something that is your job, duty, or task to deal with: It was Doug's *responsibility* to prepare the bank deposit. n. Blame, accountability, or liability for something that has happened: It was Althea's *responsibility* to make sure the alarm was set. n. Have good judgment, be dependable, reliable, or trustworthy: Increased *responsibility* usually comes with experience. *also v. response; adj. responsible*
shift	n. A group of workers who do a job for a period of time, e.g., day shift, night shift: Talia applied to work in a different department at the hospital because she did not like working the night *shift*. n. A change in position or direction: The *shift* in power happened over many years. v. A small move or change from one position or direction to another: Nicolas prefers sports car because he likes to *shift* gears.
shoplifting	n. A crime that involves taking something from a store without paying for it; stealing or thievery: *Shoplifting* is a criminal offence. v. The act of taking something from a store without paying for it: Joe was caught *shoplifting* when he was younger so he is not bondable; this means he will not be offered the cashier job that he applied for.
verify	v. Prove, confirm, validate, or make sure that something is true or correct: The front desk clerk asked to see my driver's licence so that she could *verify* the information she had on file. *also n. verification*
voluntary	adj. Given, made, or done willingly and without payment; unpaid, charitable, or intended: Participation in the game is *voluntary*. *also n. volunteer; adv. voluntarily*

Finding the Meaning

Exercise 8a

Look at the word groups. Then look at the words to the right in columns A, B, C, and D. Circle the word that has the same meaning as the word group.

WORD GROUPS	A	B	C	D
1. make sure	combination	check	cheque	fragile
2. confirm	commission	verify	shift	cheque
3. a form of payment	identification	combination	cheque	check
4. stealing	procedure	shoplifting	fragile	shift
5. scheduled time	shift	change	check	fragile
6. proof of payment	responsibility	identification	receipt	change
7. easily broken	shoplifting	procedure	reconcile	fragile
8. approval	authorization	POS terminal	receipt	shift
9. resolve	responsibility	verify	reconcile	change
10. way of doing things	identification	procedure	shift	fragile

The Right Word

Exercise 8b

Improve each sentence by replacing the highlighted word(s) with a word from the vocabulary list.

1. "Opening" the cash register may involve filling the drawer with a specific **mixture** of bills and coins so that you can make **cash returns** for the customers.

2. You should follow the store's **instructions** for closing the register at the end of your **work time** or whenever someone replaces you at the **computerized cash register**.

3. The reason for requesting **documents that prove who someone is** from a customer who is writing a **promise to pay paper** is to **prove** that the **paper payment** belongs to that customer.

4. When accepting a **paper payment**, it is the sales associate's **job** to **make sure** that the date and number amount is correct, the correct written amount is filled in and the signature and address on the **promise to pay paper** match the customer's **credentials**.

5. Credit card **authorization** may be refused because the customer has gone over the credit limit, the card has been reported stolen, a payment is overdue, or the customer has put limits on the card's use.

6. Today's **computerized cash registers** record and track customer information, process credit and debit cards, manage inventory, and lessen the chance of mistakes.

7. An important piece of information to have when **working out** sales **payments** is the sales associate's name or **recognition** number.

Apply the Meaning

Select the correct answer.

1. Which of the following does not require a **combination** of numbers to operate it?

   a) a keyless lock
   b) a locket
   c) a safe
   d) a security alarm

2. Which of the following could you **reconcile**?

   a) a large debt
   b) a walk in the park
   c) a phone number
   d) a password

3. What would you probably not use to help you **calculate** sales tax?

   a) a POS terminal
   b) a calculator
   c) your brain
   d) a cheque book

4. Two words that have the same meaning are:

   a) cheque and charge
   b) verify and check
   c) receipt and reconcile
   d) change and cheque

5. Which of the following is not a **shift**?

   a) continental
   b) days
   c) afternoons
   d) spring

6. Which job probably doesn't pay **commission**?

   a) insurance sales
   b) telemarketing
   c) janitor
   d) car sales

7. If you were eighteen years old, which product could you buy without having to show **identification**?

   a) lottery tickets
   b) condoms
   c) cigarettes
   d) alcohol

8. What type of business environment would probably not have **POS terminals**?

   a) grocery store
   b) outdoor farmer's market
   c) theatre
   d) hotel

9. Customers would be most likely to write a **cheque** if they were purchasing a new:

   a) television
   b) bedroom set
   c) dishwasher
   d) car

10. Which of the following would you probably never describe as being **fragile**?

    a) a person
    b) a diamond
    c) crystal glasses
    d) eggs

Draw a line between the letters to create words from the vocabulary list

1.   authoriza

2.   participa

                                        tion

3.   commiss

                                        ion

4.   chec

                                        ate

5.   identi

                                        ility

6.   calcul

7.   responsib   mit

8.   com   k

9.   identifica
                                        que

10. che
                                        cal

11. combina

12. accur

Fill in the Blanks: Checking Out

Fill in the blanks using the words from the word bank.

WORD BANK				
responsibility	participate	change	cheque	combination
POS terminal	verifying	check	shift	identification
authorization	fragile	receipt	procedures	outcome

The following are some low- or no-cost tips for building customer service at the _____ out counter:

1. It is the sales associates' _____ to keep the counter clean and clear throughout their _____. Checkout areas should be large, spacious, and inviting. While the counter area may be a great place to display items for sale, these items should not interfere in the checkout process. Customers need room on the counter to set their purchases, their purses, their wallets, _____ books, etc. As well, customers often will need space around the checkout area to park strollers, umbrellas, and other items while checking out.

2. Let your packaging be a walking billboard. While there is some expense involved, it's a great investment to have bold, colourful, or elegant bags with tissue paper lining and curly ribbons. Wrap the customer's purchase carefully and attractively. Wrapping a customer's purchase sets a tone, creates a quality image, and sets your business apart. Customers love it. Great packaging creates excitement for the buyer and, if it's a gift, for the recipient too. Customers like that they can have their gifts wrapped and ready to go. If the purchase is a gift and you have an assortment of tissue paper and ribbon, let the customer _____ in choosing the colour _____. People don't normally take the time to wrap cheap items, so attractive packaging makes a statement about the quality of the product inside. Remember to use extra care when wrapping _____ items.

3. You've done a great job helping the customer to select their purchases and it's now time to ring up the sale. Let the customer know what a great choice he or she has made and talk about how much the item(s) will be enjoyed while you go through the _____ on the _____, i.e., _____ the customer's _____ for a cheque or waiting for _____ on a credit card transaction, giving _____, or printing the _____. The message is that he or she is a smart consumer and a valued customer. The additional time that it takes to wrap the merchandise is also an opportunity for you to learn what other products and services your customer may be interested in. You might even end up selling something to that person that complements the purchase he or she has just made.

4. Give your customer a little lagniappe (lan-yap). The little something extra that you give should be meaningful at the moment of checkout. This should be a small item that complements the customer's purchase, like a pair of earrings from the clearance basket that match her new outfit, a few extra truffles or cookies, or a sample-size hand cream with the same scent as her new perfume. It's a very small investment that results in a very positive _____. Following these simple tips will help to brand your store in the mind of the customer.

Scanner Price Accuracy Voluntary Code

Read the passage and then answer the questions that follow it.

The Scanner Price Accuracy Voluntary Code was developed by the Retail Council of Canada, the Canadian Association of Chain Drug Stores, the Canadian Federation of Independent Grocers, and the Canadian Council of Grocery Distributors.

This Code was put into place in June 2002. It relates to all scanned Universal Product Code (UPC) , bar-coded, and/or Price Look Up (PLU) merchandise sold in all **participating** stores, with the exception of goods such as prescription drugs.

The purpose of the code is to:

- Show that retailers are **committed** to scanner price accuracy
- Provide retailers with a **consistent** way for dealing with scanner price accuracy issues
- Provide customers with a way to make a complaint if they have a problem with a retailer

The Retailers' Promise of Price Accuracy
If the scanned price of an item without a price tag is higher than the shelf price or any other displayed price, the customer is allowed to receive the item free, up to a $10 limit. When the item has a price tag, the lowest price is used. When identical items are incorrectly priced, the second one will be sold at the correct price.

What does the code cover?
The code covers all scanned merchandise at **participating** retail stores where this sign is displayed at the store entrance or checkout.

Scanning Code of Practice
If a Code of Practice problem cannot be resolved at the store level, please call 1-866-499-4599 to make your complaint.

How can I claim my refund?
- Cashiers are authorized to follow the Scanner Price Accuracy Voluntary Code.
- If you are not satisfied with the cashier's decision, you may speak to the store manager or supervisor.
- If you are still dissatisfied with the **outcome**, you may register a complaint with the Scanner Price Accuracy Committee, by calling **1-866-499-4599** (toll free).
- Your complaints and concerns will be addressed with the retailer, and you will be contacted about the **outcome**.

Comprehension Questions

Answer each question using a complete sentence.

1. Who created the Scanner Price Accuracy Voluntary Code?

    _____

    _____

2. When was the code put into place?

    _____

    _____

3. A customer is purchasing two bags of dog food. Both bags have a scanner price of $8.99, but no price tag. The customer says that the shelf price is $6.99. You have checked and the shelf price is $6.99. According to the Scanner Price Accuracy Voluntary Code, what happens now?

    _____

    _____

    _____

    _____

4. Do all stores follow the Scanner Price Accuracy Voluntary Code? Explain how you know this.

    _____

    _____

5. You are shopping at a store that has the code posted. You believe that you should receive one item for free, but the cashier refuses to honour the code. What is the next step?

    _____

    _____

6. A customer is buying two identical CDs to give as Christmas gifts to friends. The store flyer says the CDs are on sale for $10.99 each. Both CDs have a scanner price of $13.99. You have checked the flyer and the CDs are on sale this week for $10.99. According to the Scanner Price Accuracy Voluntary Code, what happens now?

    _____

    _____

    _____

Analogies: Analogies are links between words. You are looking for a relationship between the words. There is something similar or comparable about the words.

For example: grass is to green as sky is to blue

Directions: Complete each analogy by writing the correct word in the blank line.

Word Bank				
promotion	close	contest	competition	fragile
cheque	fraud	commission	prevent	key

1.   a hero is to sports as winner is to _____

2.   creator is to creation as competitor is to _____

3.   a police officer is to justice as a thief is to _____

4.   safe is to combination as door is to _____

5.   proof of purchase is to receipt as money is to _____

6.   factory worker is to wages as salesman is to _____

7.   steel is to strong as glass is to _____

8.   up is to down as open is to _____

9.   go is to proceed as stop is to _____

10.   spending is to shopping as pay raise is to _____

Review 2: Complete the Sentence
Modules 5–8

Exercise 2b

Directions: Check all the words or groups of words that can be used to make a complete correct sentence.

1. As a shoe store, our greatest competitors are

   ☐ a shoe-shine shop   ☐ department stores that sell shoes

   ☐ other shoe stores   ☐ a store that buys shoes

2. Our coupons can be used

   ☐ to the store   ☐ into the grocery store

   ☐ on weekends only   ☐ after 5:00 p.m. on Saturdays

3. The contest

   ☐ every day after school   ☐ ended on Friday

   ☐ after she wrote the book   ☐ winner today

4. I'd like to

   ☐ verify that information   ☐ exchange this ring

   ☐ show you an example   ☐ see some identification

5. What is

   ☐ Loretta demonstrating   ☐ the combination to the safe

   ☐ the promotion last week   ☐ time to close the store

6. They asked Tyler to comment

   ☐ under the weather   ☐ on the new product line

   ☐ fraud and shoplifting   ☐ role in reviewing policies

7. Refunds may be given

   ☐ at the manager's discretion   ☐ prevent fraud

   ☐ indicate a loss   ☐ require review by a manager

8. Please calculate

   ☐ Mark's commission   ☐ off for vacation

   ☐ the total of today's receipts   ☐ customer's change

Review 2: Matching
Modules 5–8

Directions: The words below have been cut in half. Match the pieces and put the answer in the space below.

tec	rtain	cou	wledge
tional	rtise	nal	oppo
cleara	uire	disc	com
adve	addi	pons	hnique
sig	ackno	unce	nce
rtunity	retion	req	petitor

1. _____
2. _____
3. _____

4. _____
5. _____
6. _____

7. _____
8. _____
9. _____

10. _____
11. _____
12. _____

Review 2: Suffixes
Modules 5–8

Which one is correct? Circle the word with the correct suffix.

1.	correct	correctment	correctly
2.	accomplish	accomplishment	accomplishly
3.	permanent	permanentment	permanently
4.	acknowledge	acknowledgement	acknowledgely
5.	additional	additionment	additionally
6.	close	closement	closely
7.	require	requirement	requirely
8.	effective	effectivement	effectively
9.	advertise	advertisement	advertisely
10.	commit	commitment	commitly
11.	neutral	neutralment	neutrally

Review 2: Antonyms
Modules 5–8

An antonym is a word that has an opposite meaning to another word. For example: hot is the opposite of cold.

Look at the words in column A. Circle a word on the same line from column B or C that is the antonym for the word in column A.

	A	B	C
1.	correct	incorrect	right
2.	classic	timeless	trendy
3.	accurate	wrong	correct
4.	combine	mix	separate
5.	famous	anonymous	recognized
6.	identical	matching	different
7.	voluntary	involuntary	unpaid
8.	neutral	biased	light-coloured
9.	fragile	delicate	tough
10.	consistent	dependable	inconsistent
11.	additional	extra	less
12.	authorize	prevent	allow

MODULE NINE

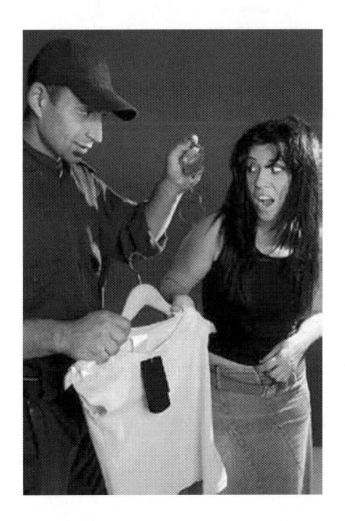

PREVENTING LOSS

VOCABULARY—Module 9

account	n. An agreement with a bank to hold your money for you, allowing you to deposit and withdraw money when you need to: When I moved to Windsor, I opened a savings *account* with a credit union. n. A spoken or written description of an event; explanation, story, report, or version: Her *account* of the accident is different from his. n. An agreement with a store or company that lets you buys things and pay for them later; credit, tab, or bill: I asked the hotel to charge the massage and all of my meals to my *account*.
accuse	v. To say that someone has done something wrong, illegal, or unkind; blame, point the finger at, or hold responsible: Vida's doctor was *accused* of negligence. *also n. accusation*
administrative	adj. The arrangements and work which are needed to control a business, company, venture, setup, process, action, or procedure: Linda was given a list of *administrative* tasks to complete. *also v. administer; n. administrator; n. administration; adv. administratively*
apparel	n. Clothing, attire, garb: Liz sells *apparel* in a secondhand store.
arrest	v. To be taken away by the police to answer questions about a crime that may have been committed; to take into custody, seize, capture, detain, catch, hold, apprehend, pick up, or stop: Jake was *arrested* for drinking and driving. v. To stop something; halt, stop, block, prevent, obstruct, impede, or check: They were unable to *arrest* the spread of the disease. n. When the police take someone away to ask that person about a crime he or she may have committed; capture, seizure, or detention: An *arrest* was made in connection to the armed robbery at the bank.
average	n. The result of adding two or more amounts together and dividing the total by the number of amounts, e.g., the *average* of 5+3+4+4 is 4 because the total of the four numbers (16) divided by the amount of numbers (4) is 4. n. Typical, usual, standard, regular, normal, common, or ordinary: On *average*, I work fifty hours per week. v. Be around; be an approximation of; be more or less: I *average* 20 miles per week on my bike. adj. math formula: The *average* age of school dropouts is 16. adj. Typical/usual: The *average* person visits 59 websites a month.

conceal	v. To hide something or prevent something from being seen or known about; cover up, mask, camouflage, cloak, or disguise: The young man tried to *conceal* the CD inside his jacket.
confront	v. Face up to or deal with a difficult person or situation; challenge someone; tackle, face up to, meet head-on, meet, face, deal with, challenge, threaten, or defy: The sales associate had to *confront* an older woman about stealing a package of gum earlier today. *also n. confrontation; adj. confrontational*
detain	v. To force someone to stay in a place; delay someone for a short time; arrest, hold, keep in custody, capture, confine, control, restrain, delay, hold up, or keep: I'm sorry to *detain* you Mr. Boss, but could you please sign my pay cheque before you leave. The girl was *detained* by the police at the scene of the accident because she had been drinking.
deter	v. Discourage, put off, prevent, frighten, or threaten someone in order to stop them from doing something: The new security tags help to *deter* shoplifters.
error	n. A mistake, fault, slipup, inaccuracy, miscalculation, or blunder: Forgetting to charge customers for large products that are sitting on the bottom of the shopping cart is a serious employee *error* that can cost a company a lot of money.
examine	v. To look at or consider something or someone carefully in order to discover something about them; inspect, scrutinize, observe, study, or scan: I need to *examine* the problem more closely. The doctor will *examine* my ears to make sure that my hearing is normal. v. Test someone's knowledge or skill; assess, analyze, appraise, weigh, research, investigate, consider, or look into: The teacher said we would be *examined* twice in the next year. *also n. examination; n. examiner*
expensive	adj. Costing a lot of money; pricey, high-priced, dear, luxurious, classy, posh, or exclusive: Gideon bought Jessica a very *expensive* diamond ring for their anniversary. *also n. expense*
internal	adj. Happening or existing inside an object, organization, place, person, or country; interior, inner, inside, domestic, in-house, or home: The accident caused the man to have *internal* injuries. The company will be posting several *internal* job openings. *adv. internally*

population	n. All of the people who live in a particular area, place, city, or country; inhabitants or residents: More than 70% of the *population* in North America uses the Internet.
promptly	adv. On time, punctually, at the appointed time, quickly, rapidly, swiftly, without delay, or speedily: He arrived *promptly* at 1:00 p.m. *also v. prompt; adj. prompt; n. prompt*
security	n. Protection against crimes or attacks; safety, sanctuary, defence, safekeeping, protection, precautions, or well-being: *Security* is about protecting people, places, and things from danger, damage, loss, and criminal activity. *also v. secure; adj. secure; adv. securely*
shrinkage	n. Reduction, decrease, or decline: The loss suffered by stores due to theft and employee error is referred to as *shrinkage*.
survey	n. To find out opinions, behaviour, etc. by asking people questions; review, study, examination, investigation, inspection, assessment, analysis, appraisal, scrutiny, or evaluation: According to a *survey* conducted by Statistics Canada, 53% of adults participate in at least thirty minutes of physical activity one or more days a week. n. The measuring and recording of the details about an area of land: We gave a copy of our property *survey* to the construction company. v. To look at or examine something carefully; review, study, examine, investigate, inspect, assess, analyze, appraise, scrutinize, evaluate, or consider: The insurance adjuster said he would have to *survey* the damage to our house before he could make a decision. v. To ask people questions to find out their opinions, behaviours, etc.: They will *survey* the staff for their opinion about the new policies.
suspect	n. Somebody who might be guilty: They have arrested a *suspect*. v. Think, believe, suppose, expect, imagine, guess, deduce, or infer: I *suspect* that he will be retiring next year. v. To believe that somebody is guilty or committed a crime or wrongdoing, without any proof: They *suspect* him of stealing?
target	n. Aim, goal, or objective: Their *target* was the toy store in the mall. n. An object that is shot at during shooting practice: I took five shots, but never hit the *target*. v. Aim at, go for, point, steer, direct at, or be after: Shoplifters often *target* designer merchandise to steal.

theft	n. The taking and keeping of something that doesn't belong to you; robbery, stealing, shoplifting, burglary, larceny, or pilfering: The *theft* of expensive cars has increased over the past year. *also n. thief*
witness	n. A person who sees something happen, usually a crime or an accident; an observer, bystander, or eyewitness: The security guard asked the *witness* for a description of the three boys. v. To see, observe, or view something that happens: Did Ljubomir *witness* the accident?

Finding the Meaning

Look at the word groups. Then look at the words to the right in columns A, B, C, and D. Circle the word that has the same meaning as the word group.

	WORD GROUPS	A	B	C	D
1.	someone who sees a crime happen	witness	suspect	theft	security
2.	right away	target	promptly	accuse	error
3.	getting smaller	shrinkage	expensive	promptly	deter
4.	a mistake	error	deter	security	profitable
5.	protection	profitable	witness	theft	security
6.	to believe something	witness	deter	suspect	confront
7.	deal with	promptly	confront	detain	accuse
8.	cover up	conceal	confront	profitable	suspect
9.	slow down	confront	accuse	deter	detain
10.	aim at	deter	expensive	target	detain

Improve each sentence by replacing the highlighted word(s) with a word from the vocabulary list.

1. A store would be most likely to use an electronic cable to prevent theft of a **high-priced** leather coat.

2. If you **think** someone is trying to **hide** store merchandise, but haven't personally **seen** any sign of **stealing**, you cannot **point a finger at** the person of shoplifting.

3. Sales associates contribute to loss prevention in their stores when they report stock **reduction**.

4. Package switching is a type of **stealing** where the thief **masks** a higher-priced item in the box of a lower-priced item, pays the lower price, and leaves the store.

5. Falsely **blaming** someone of shoplifting could result in injury to someone trying to **confine** the **possibly guilty person**.

6. In order to **face up to** or **confine** someone for shoplifting, you must personally **observe** an individual picking up the item, **covering up** the item, and leaving the store without planning to pay for the item.

7. As a sales associate, you have knowledge of possible **safety** problems in your area. By warning management about major **decrease in stock** threats, a decision may be made to change the layout of the department to reduce or prevent future **pilfering**.

Apply the Meaning

Select the correct answer.

1. Which of the following is not an **error**?

   a) biting your nails
   c) a wrong answer
   b) a typing mistake
   d) bouncing a cheque

2. A person who has been **detained** by their boss is probably:

   a) on vacation
   c) shopping
   b) at work
   d) on a date

3. Which of the following would probably not be a **target** for theft?

   a) a church
   c) a walking trail
   b) a library
   d) a restaurant

4. Which of the following would probably not be **profitable**?

   a) selling jewellery
   c) losing your job
   b) winning the lottery
   d) investing in gold

5. What is something you might **suspect**?

   a) you had lunch with your sister
   b) your friend is pregnant

   c) you received a job offer last week
   d) you paid your credit card bill last month

6. Which one of the following types of **theft** is not fraud?

   a) writing a bad cheque
   c) counterfeit money
   b) shoplifting
   d) stolen credit cards

7. Which of the following would you use to **conceal** a pimple?

   a) a mask
   c) a hat
   b) makeup
   d) wallpaper

8. Which of the following is probably not something you would **accuse** someone of:

   a) gift-giving
   c) stealing
   b) cheating
   d) over-spending

9. Which of the following would not be **expensive**?

   a) a television
   c) a car
   b) a house
   d) a walk

10. You could be a **witness** if …

    a) you did something wrong
    c) you invited someone for dinner
    b) you saw something happen
    d) you told a funny story

Study the Words: Suffixes   Exercise 9d

A suffix is an ending that is added to a word to create a new word. The new words are similar in meaning to the original word, but they are different parts of speech.

The following words are formed by adding suffixes to the word administer.

		Meaning
1.	administer	v. To control the operation or arrangement of something v. To cause someone to receive something
2.	administrative	adj. Relating to the arrangements and work which is needed to control the operation of a plan or organization
3.	administrator	n. Someone whose job is to control the operation of a business, organization, or plan
4.	administration	n. The arrangements and tasks needed to control the operation of a plan or organization n. When someone is given something

Fill in the blanks below using the correct form of the word **administer**.

1. There are three junior executives on the board of directors who
_____ the summer camp project.

2. You must notify the _____ regarding any changes to the
proposal.

3. David's _____ duties include organizing events, arranging
travel for his boss, and ordering supplies.

4. The shareholders do not hold much control of the day-to-day
_____ of the company's operations.

5. You must _____ the medication to the patient once every
three hours for seven days.

6. The _____ of client medications can be very time-consuming.

Fill in the Blanks: Loss Prevention   Exercise 9e

Fill in the blanks using the words from the word bank.

WORD BANK				
survey	security	apparel	theft	errors
promptly	administrative	deter	shrinkage	suspect
security	concealed	examine	expensive	witnessed

Procedures to help reduce _____:

1. Someone should be on the sales floor at all times to assist customers and help

    _____ _____. When walking the floor,

    _____ everything carefully and _____ respond to:

- ☐ mismarked _____ or other merchandise
- ☐ incorrect pricing
- ☐ loose price tickets
- ☐ unlocked _____ fixtures
- ☐ open showcases
- ☐ empty packages
- ☐ known shoplifters or suspicious customers
- ☐ merchandise _____ for later pickup
- ☐ _____ merchandise without security tags
- ☐ broken _____ equipment
- ☐ salespeople not following _____ procedures
- ☐ cashiers not properly ringing in sales, or other cash _____.
- ☐ coupons procedures not being followed
- ☐ loose bags or gift boxes that are accessible to customers
- ☐ customers not being served
- ☐ merchandise under the counter that has not been paid for
- ☐ employee handbags or backpacks under counters
- ☐ unauthorized cheques, voids, or refunds

2. Employees should greet or acknowledge every customer who enters the store.
3. Provide personal customer service to as many customers as possible.
4. Employees should make frequent eye contact with customers who are just looking.
5. Staff can _____ assigned zones so that at risk areas aren't left unattended.
6. Employees should alert another staff member or manager if they
    _____ or have _____ a theft.

Protecting Company Assets

Read the passage and then answer the questions that follow it.

The Centre for Retail Research produced a report that examines retail theft around the world. They surveyed 1,103 retailers in forty-two countries. Their report, *The 2010 Global Retail Theft Barometer*, found that the total amount of **shrinkage** for retailers around the world came to $107.3 billion (1.36% of sales). The global cost of this crime is $185.59 per family. The countries with the highest shrink rates are India, Morocco, and Brazil. The countries with the lowest shrink rates are Austria, Hong Kong, and Taiwan. Retailers around the world spent $26.8 billion on loss-prevention strategies in an effort to **deter** theft. Approximately 6.2 million shoplifters and employee thieves were arrested in 2010—more than the population of many countries.

Shoplifting
- Shoplifting is the number one cause of **shrinkage** for retailers around the world.
- Shoplifting accounts for $45.5 billion in merchandise **shrinkage** (42.4% of total shrinkage).
- On average, a shoplifter takes $196.00 worth of goods per visit.

Employee **Theft**
- Employee theft is the second-largest cause of **shrinkage** at $37.8 billion (35.3%).
- Employees steal an average of $1,944.00—almost ten times more than shoplifters.
- There are, however, more shoplifters than there are employee thieves.

Internal **Error** and Administrative Failure
- Pricing or accounting mistakes caused shrinkage of $18.1 billion (16.9%).

Supplier or Vendor Fraud/**Theft**
- Overcharging retailers for merchandise or sending fewer items than what have been paid for caused shrinkage of $5.8 billion (5.4%).

The highest shrink is found in branded and **expensive** products. The items most **targeted** are:
- Apparel high-risk product lines: accessories and children's wear
- Grocery high-risk product lines: fresh meat and luxury cooked meat
- Health and beauty high-risk product lines: shaving products and perfumes/fragrances
- Other high shrink items include easily-**concealed** merchandise like razor blades, DVDs/CDs, video games, and small electric items.

Comprehension Questions

Answer each question using a complete sentence.

1. What is shrinkage?

   _____

   _____

2. Where do the statistics for this passage come from?

   _____

   _____

3. What is the number one cause of shrinkage and how much does it cost retailers?

   _____

   _____

4. Name two high-shrink items.

   _____

   _____

5. What is vendor fraud?

   _____

   _____

6. Which countries have the lowest shrink rates?

   _____

   _____

7. How many countries participated in the survey?

   _____

   _____

8. What is the second-largest cause of shrinkage and how much does it cost retailers?

   _____

   _____

MODULE TEN

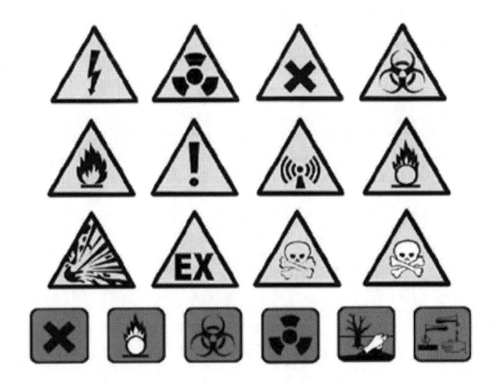

PROMOTING
WORKPLACE SAFETY

VOCABULARY—Module 10

affect	v. To have an influence on something or someone or cause them to change; have an effect on, influence, involve, shape, concern, change, distress, touch, disturb, move, upset, or have an emotional impact on: If you get a divorce, it will *affect* all parts of your life. v. To pretend to think or feel something; assume, pretend to have, put on, imitate, or fake: When they fired her, she was able to *affect* indifference.
alert	v. Warn, notify, tell, or inform someone of possible danger: Kurt called to *alert* the department manager about the accident. n. A warning, signal, or alarm that tells people of possible danger: The supervisor sounded the evacuation *alert* at 2:45 a.m. adj. Quick to see, understand, and act in a situation: Tyler felt wide awake and *alert* after the surgery.
assign	v. To give a job or piece of work to someone; allocate, allot, give, dispense, consign, or hand over: The teacher will *assign* homework later today. v. To send someone somewhere to do a job; delegate or designate: Don't *assign* Derek to any out-of-town projects for the next few weeks. v. To give property, money, or rights using a legal process; delegate, send, name, allocate, designate, or transfer: *Assign* the money to your son. *also n. assignment*
awkward	adj. Bulky or difficult to move, use, or deal with: The proper way to lift a heavy or *awkward* item is to use your knees rather than your back. adj. Feeling uncomfortable, embarrassed, tongue-tied, or self-conscious: It was a very *awkward* moment when she told him in front of all of us that she didn't want to see him anymore. adj. Clumsy or uncoordinated; moving in an unattractive way: She's much too *awkward* to be a dancer. *also n. awkwardness; adv. awkwardly*
barrier	n. A fence, wall, or barricade that stops people from going somewhere: The workers put up a *barrier* to block off the construction area. n. An obstacle, hurdle, or difficulty; something that stops people from being together or understanding each other: The stairs are a *barrier* for the man with the walker. When Mark first moved to Canada, language was a *barrier* for him.

carton	n. A box or container made from thick cardboard or plastic, used for storing things: Bill used a fork lift to move the large *cartons* outside.
concern	n. Worry, fear, alarm, anxiety, or distress: Linda's biggest *concern* was that she might not be able to help the lady who was crying on the phone. n. Something that is important to you: There is a matter of great *concern* that I need to speak with Emma about. n. When you feel worried or nervous about something: My *concern* is that you are not getting your work done quickly enough. v. Relate to, affect, involve, or be about: This discussion doesn't *concern* you. v. To worry: It *concerns* me that Victor hasn't called yet.
coordinate	v. To make different things work well together; organize, direct, manage, synchronize, or bring together: Pat will *coordinate* the charity fundraiser. v. To match or look attractive together; synchronize, harmonize, or match up: She will *coordinate* her winter wardrobe while she is on holidays. *also n. coordination; n. coordinator*
co-worker	n. Someone you work with; fellow worker, associate, or colleague: My *co-workers* spent three weeks writing the new safety policy.
goggles	n. Safety glasses; spectacles or eyeglasses that are made especially to protect the eyes from chemicals, wind, water, etc.: The company policy states that anyone working in this area must wear safety *goggles*.
hazardous	adj. Dangerous, risky, unsafe, or harmful: *Hazardous* materials are solids, liquids, or gases that can hurt or kill you.
income	n. Money earned from working or making investments; pay, wage, salary, earnings, profits, or revenue: He earns a high *income* as a lawyer.
injury	n. Physical harm, hurt, wrong, damage, or wound caused by an accident or attack: Grace has been unable to work since her back *injury*.
inspect	v. To look at someone or something carefully in order to find information, usually about quality or condition; examine, check, scrutinize, look over, or study: They will *inspect* our store security system on Friday. *also n. inspector; n. inspection*
occupation	n. A person's job, profession, work, career, livelihood, living, employment, or regular activity: Patti's *occupation* is listed as sales associate. n. When an army or group moves in and takes control of a place: He

	survived the *occupation* of his country and moved here as a refugee. *also v. occupy; adj. occupational; adj. occupied*
operate	v. To work; be moving or have an effect; function, run, activate, control, drive, manoeuvre, manage, organize, conduct, or direct: How do you *operate* the remote for the television? v. (medical) To cut a body open to repair, remove, or replace a damaged or diseased part: Do they plan to *operate* on him today? *also n. operation; adj. operational*
overloaded	adj. Supplied with too much/too many of something: The *overloaded* shelves were about to collapse. v. To put too large or heavy a load on somebody or something or in something; too much work, stress, or other difficulty; weighed down, loaded, burdened: The safety committee reported that the shelves were *overloaded* with stock and that the power bar was a safety risk because it was *overloaded* with computer cords.
protect	v. To keep someone or something safe from loss, injury, or damage; defend, guard, keep, look after, care for, save from harm, shield, shelter, safeguard, or watch over: A warm coat and boots will *protect* you from the cold. *also n. protection; adj. protective*
safety	n. Security, protection, shelter, or well-being: For the *safety* of everyone working at the mall, the janitor put in a bright light near the employee entrance. *also n. safe; adj. safe*
shelf	n. (plural: shelves) A flat place or ledge to store or display things that can be attached to a wall or be part of a cabinet: It is Nazir's job to stock the large metal *shelves* in the showroom with pet food. Please put the candles on the top *shelf*.
stepladder	n. A folding ladder that has wide, flat steps and a hinged frame: Florence was told not to climb the *stepladder* with high-heeled shoes on.
visible	adj. Able to be seen, noticeable, evident, or obvious: There should be a *visible* exit sign at the front and back of the store. *also n. visibility; adv. visibly*

Finding the Meaning

Look at the word groups. Then look at the words to the right in columns A, B, C, and D. Circle the word that has the same meaning as the word group.

	WORD GROUPS	A	B	C	D
1.	watchful	awkward	shelf	visible	alert
2.	able to be seen	concern	visible	barrier	alert
3.	difficult to move	awkward	barrier	safety	goggles
4.	a fence	co-worker	injury	cartons	barrier
5.	boxes	visible	hazardous	cartons	shelf
6.	something to cover your eyes	hazardous	goggles	shelf	safety
7.	harm	safety	injury	income	alert
8.	worry or fear	overloaded	awkward	injury	concern
9.	earnings	barrier	co-worker	safety	income
10.	protection	safety	income	awkward	injury

The Right Word

Improve each sentence by replacing the highlighted word(s) with a word from the vocabulary list.

1. An example of a **dangerous** condition is a **ledge** that is **weighed down** with heavy boxes.

2. The money a company spends as a result of accidents may result in less **wages** and benefits for employees.

3. If a customer spills water on the floor, the first thing you should do is block off the area with a **fence**.

4. When a customer asks for merchandise on a high shelf, the sales associate should use a **staircase on hinges**.

5. If **boxes** containing heavy appliances fall on the floor, a sales associate should put up a **small wall** and **notify** management.

6. An important part of maintaining **well-being** in the workplace is acting to correct **harmful** conditions as soon as possible.

7. You should never feel **embarrassed** about sharing **fears** about **protection** with your manager or **colleagues**.

Apply the Meaning

Select the correct answer.

1. A person might use **goggles** for all of these activities except:

    a) skiing
    b) swimming
    c) welding
    d) dieting

2. Which of the following is not an **injury**?

    a) a broken leg
    b) a cold
    c) a cut
    d) a burn

3. Which of the following is sometimes not **visible** at night when you live in a city?

    a) ghostly spirits
    b) the stars
    c) the sun
    d) buildings

4. An **awkward** moment might be:

    a) meeting your sister for lunch
    b) taking your dog for a walk
    c) meeting your in-laws for the first time
    d) waiting in line at the grocery store

5. What do people usually not store on garage **shelves**?

    a) golf clubs
    b) boxes
    c) junk
    d) food

6. What would you probably not use a **stepladder** for?

    a) changing a light bulb
    b) a children's climber
    c) painting a house
    d) cleaning windows

7. At which job would you probably not have **co-workers**?

    a) factory worker
    b) bank teller
    c) retail clerk
    d) babysitter

8. Which of the following may not provide a steady **income**?

    a) tradesman
    b) gambler
    c) security guard
    d) doctor

9. What does an amber **alert** mean?

    a) there's been a car accident
    b) there's a fire in the building
    c) a child is missing
    d) slow down for construction

10. Wet floors can be **hazardous** because someone walking on them could:

    a) get electrocuted
    b) slip and fall
    c) get very wet
    d) get a fever

Study the Words: Affect/Effect

Study the meaning of the words below and then complete the exercise that follows.

		Meaning
1.	affect	v. To influence someone or something: Smoking *affects* your health. v. To pretend or imitate: The actor *affected* a British accent.
2.	effect	n. A result or consequence that was caused or brought about: The changes to the teaching staff had an immediate *effect* on the students' behaviour.

Fill in the blanks below using the proper forms of the words **affect** or **effect.**

1. Possible side- _____ include nausea and drowsiness.

2. Changing schools had no apparent _____ on our daughter's progress.

3. The new manager had an excellent _____ on the attitude of the staff.

4. We were worried that moving during the school year would _____ her progress.

5. Nothing seems to _____ his appetite.

6. There are many factors that _____ the sale of merchandise in a store.

7. The study looked at the _____ of commuting time on work performance.

8. Many people were _____ by the tsunami, especially those who were living in the areas that were hit the worst.

9. The new medication had a positive _____ on her energy level.

10. Winning $25 million _____ all aspects of Pat's life.

Fill in the Blanks: Retail Safety Checklist   Exercise 10e

Fill in the blanks using the words from the word bank.

WORD BANK					
hazardous	barriers	cartons	concern	protected	inspected
injury	inspect	goggles	stepladders	co-worker	barriers
overloaded	operators	safety	shelves	visible	awkward

_____ all areas for _____ and consider the points listed below. Use a "√" to indicate that an item is okay. Use an "X" to indicate that there is a _____.

☐ Aisles and doorways are clear of materials, equipment, or other _____.

☐ Floors are clean, dry, and free of oil or grease; carpets or tiles are in good condition

☐ Goods stored on the floor are clear of doors/aisles and are stacked no more than three _____ high.

☐ _____ are safe, have anti-slip treads, and are in good condition.

☐ Stairwells are clear of materials, equipment, or other _____.

☐ Stairs and handrails are secure and in good condition; stairs have anti-slip treads.

☐ Lighting levels are adequate; work areas are free of glare or excessive lighting contrast.

☐ Windows are covered with blinds, drapes, or other means of controlling light.

☐ Electrical cords, plugs, sockets, and switches are secured and in good condition.

☐ There is clear access to electrical panels.

☐ Supplies and materials are stored properly on _____ and positioned for safe lifting.

☐ Floors around the shelves are clear of garbage.

☐ Racks and shelves are in good condition and not _____.

☐ Trolleys or dollies are available to move heavy or _____ items.

☐ Equipment is kept clean and regularly maintained; _____ are properly trained.

☐ Chairs are properly adjusted and in good condition.

☐ Computer display screens are bright and positioned at a comfortable viewing level.

☐ Fire extinguishers are clearly marked and properly installed on the walls.

☐ Fire extinguishers have been_____ within the year; workers are trained to use them.

☐ Emergency phone numbers are close to the phone(s) and are _____.

☐ Smoke, fire, and burglar alarms are in place.

☐ Emergency exits are clear; emergency exit signs and lighting units are working.

☐ The first-aid kit is accessible and clearly labelled; the kit is adequate and complete, clean, and dry.

☐ Accident report forms are accessible; in case of an _____, emergency numbers are displayed.

☐ Material _____ Data Sheets (MSDS) are provided for all dangerous materials.

☐ Workers are _____ from cool drafts/excessive heat and excessive/irritating noise.

☐ Parking areas are safe and appropriately lighted (names should not be painted on spots).

☐ Workers are encouraged to walk in the parking lot with a _____ or friend.

☐ Garbage bins are located at suitable points and emptied regularly.

☐ Workers know where to go and whom to call for first-aid assistance.

☐ Workers know how to locate and use personal protective equipment (e.g., gloves, _____).

Safety is Everyone's Business

Read the passage and then answer the questions that follow it.

ABC's of safety: **A**lways **B**e **C**areful

Safety is the responsibility of the:
Employer—Supervisor—Worker

Employer Responsibilities:
- Provide a workplace that is safe and healthy.
- Make sure workers are properly trained; follow up to see that the supervisor is carrying out all required training.
- Record who has received training, including the completion date and type of training.
- Set up and maintain an occupational health and safety program, including a procedure for incident investigation and a policy for health and safety.
- Support supervisors, safety coordinators, and workers in their health and safety activities.
- Take action right away when a worker or supervisor reports a potentially **hazardous** situation.
- Start an investigation into incidents.
- Advise your local Workers' Compensation Office of any serious incidents.
- Provide workers with personal protective equipment as required.
- Make sure there are enough first-aid facilities and services.

Supervisor Responsibilities:
- Provide an orientation and training to workers in safe work procedures.
- Ensure that safety training is provided to workers for all work-related tasks.
- Make sure that workers who are operating tools and equipment or using hazardous chemicals are authorized and properly training.
- Ensure the proper handling, storing and maintenance of all equipment and materials.
- Make sure that all health and **safety** requirements are enforced (e.g., wearing **goggles** in particular work areas).
- Resolve any unsafe acts and conditions.
- Identify workers with problems that could potentially affect workplace safety.
- Follow up with interviews and referrals where necessary.
- Create rules for health and safety and inspect the site for workplace hazards.

Worker Responsibilities:
- Know and follow health and safety requirements affecting your job.
- Make sure you have the necessary training before you start a task.
- Work safely, and encourage your **co-workers** to do the same.
- Fix or stop any unsafe situations or report them to your supervisor straight away.
- Report any **injury** without delay to a first-aid attendant or supervisor.
- Take the initiative. Make suggestions to improve health and **safety**.

True or False

		True	False
1.	Business is business; the supervisor's first priority is to make sure that everyone is working fast enough to get the job done regardless of any safety issues.	☐	☐
2.	Workers should pay attention to their own safety on the job and not worry about anyone else.	☐	☐
3.	It is the worker's responsibility to know and follow health and safety requirements that affect their job.	☐	☐
4.	It is the worker's responsibility to ensure that equipment and materials are properly handled, stored, and maintained.	☐	☐
5.	Workers should not report any unsafe conditions because it's the supervisor's job to walk around, observe, and fix these things.	☐	☐
6.	Employers are responsible for making sure that there are written records of all the health and safety training activities that their staff participate in.	☐	☐
7.	Someone with a drinking problem could affect safety at a worksite.	☐	☐
8.	It is the worker's responsibility to create health and safety rules.	☐	☐
9.	If an employee doesn't know how to do a job safely, that person should complain to their co-workers.	☐	☐
10.	It is the employer's responsibility to reports serious accidents to the local Workers' Compensation Office.	☐	☐

Crossword: Promoting Safety

Across

1. able to be seen
8. a synonym for boxes
11. to organize or manage people or things
12. to have an influence on something
14. to inform someone of possible danger

Down

2. damage that is caused by an accident
3. feeling uncomfortable or embarrassed
4. money that you earn from working
5. to look at something very carefully
6. something that stops people from going somewhere
7. safety glasses
9. a person's job
10. dangerous or unsafe
12. to give a job to someone
13. a flat place to store or display things

Don't be afraid to ask a dumb question. It's a lot easier to deal with than a dumb mistake.

MODULE ELEVEN

STOCKING THE SHELVES

VOCABULARY—Module 11

conscious	adj. To notice that someone or something is present or exists; aware, mindful, or cognizant: Debbie is *conscious* of the fact that she does not have the leadership skills needed to do the job.
	adj. Awake, alert, or aware; thinking and knowing what is happening around you: Lendon was seriously injured in the accident, but he's still *conscious*.
	adj. Intentional, deliberate, premeditated, on purpose, or determined: Devon is making a *conscious* effort to be nice to his co-workers.
	also adv. consciously; n. consciousness; n. subconscious; adj. subconscious
consumer	n. A person who buys goods or services for their own use; customer, user, shopper, buyer, patron, or purchaser: They did a survey of local *consumers* and decided it was a good idea to build another grocery store.
	also n. consumerism
convenient	adj. Suitable for your purposes and needs; causing the least difficulty; expedient, opportune, fitting, handy, well-located, or well-situated: Our store offers a *convenient* location, as well as *convenient* hours.
	also n. convenience; adv. conveniently
cosmetics	n. Beauty products that you put on your face or body to help improve its appearance; makeup, foundation, eye shadow, mascara, lipstick, or perfume: Jhira's favourite part of the drug store is the *cosmetics* area.
customize	v. To make or change something according to the person's needs; modify, tailor, adapt, make to order, make specially, or convert: Derek plans to *customize* his car with graphic designs.
	also n. custom; n. customization
dispense	v. Give things out to people, e.g., products, medication, services, amounts of money; hand out, distribute, dole out, allot, or bestow: The nurses *dispense* the medication to the patients at 4:00 p.m. every day.
	also n. dispenser; adj. dispensable; n. dispensary
essential	adj. Necessary, vital, important, critical, key, basic, or fundamental: Making sure there is enough inventory for a sale is an *essential* part of providing good customer service.
	n. A basic thing you cannot live without; necessary, vital, or important: We can only take the bare *essentials* to the island.
	also adv. essentially

expiration	n. When something ends or stops being in use; run out, finish, conclusion, or termination: The bananas were on sale because they had passed their *expiration* date. *also v. expire*
inventory	n. A list, record, account, or catalogue of all the things in a place: After Halloween the store's entire *inventory* of masks sold for 50% off.
invest	v. To put time, money, and effort into making a profit or getting an advantage; spend, devote, advance, endow, provide, supply, empower, or authorize: There are three businesses that plan to *invest* in the new self-serve project. *also n. investment; n. investor*
monitor	v. To watch or check a situation carefully to find something out about it; check, watch, observe, keep an eye on, supervise, or examine: The girl who is supposed to *monitor* the fitting rooms is on break. n. A person who has the job of watching or noticing particular things: The hall *monitor* sent the students back to class. n. A screen on which words or pictures can be shown: We bought a new computer *monitor*.
organize	v. Put in order, sort out, arrange, manage, coordinate, control, fix, take charge of, or make plans for: It took days to *organize* the new store. *also n. organization; adj. organizational; n. organizer*
packing slip	n. Delivery list; a document that lists the contents of a package, usually inside or attached to the outside of the package: The *packing slip* said that there were twenty t-shirts in each of the three boxes.
perishable	adj. Describes food that can rot quickly; easily ruined or broken, not preserved, fresh, consumable, delicate, or fragile: She has a full basket of *perishable* food items to put back in the coolers. *also v. perish*
purchase order	n. A paper that tells one business what another business would like to buy, i.e., the number, sizes, and agreed prices: Ana sent a *purchase order* to the manufacturer requesting ten more beds for the hospital.
rotate	v. To turn in a circle around a fixed point; turn, go around, revolve, spin, take turns, or replace: The wheel on the truck *rotates* around an axle. Farmers *rotate* their crops. My father will *rotate* onto the night shift next week. *also n. rotation*

routine	n. A usual way of doing things: It's the same *routine* every day. adj. Done as part of what usually happens, e.g., a routine inspection; custom, habit, practice, regular, everyday, standard, normal, dull, boring, monotonous, tedious, repetitive: Jennifer went for a *routine* check-up.
scanner	n. A tool used to track inventory: Bar-code *scanners* are used in all types industries, e.g., libraries, education, entertainment, retail, hospitality, manufacturing, warehousing: He used a bar-code *scanner* to see how many more cartons of paper they had left in the warehouse.
seasonal	adj. Happening at particular times of year or period of time, e.g., Christmas, Easter, Valentine's Day, Thanksgiving, winter, summer, spring, or fall: I enjoy creating the *seasonal* displays at work. *also n. season*
transfer	v. To move, remove, shift, relocate, send on, pass on, hand over, sign over, or turn over something or someone from one place, person, or group to another: Please *transfer* the winter stock to the warehouse. n. Relocate or reassign: I was given a *transfer* to the other store. n. A travel ticket which allows someone to change from one bus or train to another: I have to *transfer* buses three times in order to get to work. *also adj. transferable; n. transference*
UPC	Universal Product Code: *UPC* codes help to keep track of inventory.
variation	n. A difference, distinction, discrepancy, alternative, or type, e.g., colour, size, or model: There are several *variations* of the new sunglasses on display. n. A change in amount or level: Although there were some *variations* in temperature throughout the week, we had a wonderful holiday. *also v. vary; adj. various; adj. variable; n. variable; n. variability*
vendor	n. Someone who is selling something; a seller, salesperson, trader, merchant, retailer, wholesaler, hawker, dealer, purveyor, or peddler: The *vendor* spent all day on the beach selling his crafts. *also n. vending*
wholesale	adv. The selling of goods in large amounts at low prices to stores and businesses rather than in stores or to customers: We sell *wholesale* cleaning products to many factories in the area. n. The price at which goods are sold to shops by the people who make them rather than the price that the customer pays: I bought a new car *wholesale* at the factory.

Finding the Meaning

Look at the word groups. Then look at the words to the right in columns A, B, C, and D. Circle the word that has the same meaning as the word group.

WORD GROUPS	A	B	C	D
1. something that is necessary	cosmetics	essential	seasonal	scanner
2. you use a scanner to read these numbers and lines	NHL	POS	UPC	UPS
3. a type of product that is sold at a certain time of the year	seasonal	stock	organize	inventory
4. move something to a different place	transfer	scanner	variations	vendor
5. something that needs to be eaten before it goes bad	cosmetics	perishable	seasonal	stock
6. items to improve the way you look	inventory	cosmetics	scanner	vendor
7. someone who sells things	vendor	organize	variations	stock
8. put into order	seasonal	cosmetics	organize	vendor
9. watching or checking on something or someone	perishable	monitoring	variations	inventory
10. a date when something ends	seasonal	expiration	organize	vendor

Improve each sentence by replacing the highlighted word(s) with a word from the vocabulary list.

1. The **supervising** of **stock items** is an **important** part of providing excellent customer service.

2. **Stock** items that cannot be fixed or resold by your store may be given to charity, thrown in the garbage, **passed on** to a discount store, or returned to the **wholesaler**.

3. If you are responsible for restocking **fresh** items, remember that it is **crucial** to place the newer products at the back of the shelf and move the ones that are close to their **end** dates toward the front so that they will be purchased first.

4. A **detailed list of items that has been requested from a vendor** was sent to your office by fax on Friday.

5. A **paper that lists the items that have been shipped** was included in the box.

6. When Lisa **sorted out** the **beauty products** in her department she made sure that there were several **alternatives** of each product.

7. The **wholesaler** asked the new sales assistant to use the **tracking tool** to check the **list** of **certain time of year** products their store had on hand.

Apply the Meaning

Select the correct answer.

1. Which **vendor** would probably supply restaurants with alcoholic beverages?

   a) The Fruit Guy
   c) Barn's Winery
   b) Jonathan's Nuts
   d) Meg's Desserts

2. Which one of the following is probably not a type of **transfer**?

   a) baby transfer
   c) bus transfer
   b) money transfer
   d) job transfer

3. Which one of the following is a **perishable** item?

   a) detergent
   c) tissue paper
   b) milk
   d) jewellery

4. Which of the following is probably not a good reason for **monitoring** inventory?

   a) lets you see how well a product is selling
   c) helps you to know what is in stock at any time
   b) it helps to keep staff busy
   d) alerts you to when it's time to reorder items

5. Where would you probably not find an **expiration** date?

   a) licence
   c) passport
   b) birth certificate
   d) credit card

6. How would you most likely send a **purchase order**?

   a) by fax
   c) in person
   b) by air mail
   d) by courier

7. Which one of the following is not a **cosmetics** product?

   a) lip gloss
   c) body spray
   b) nail polish
   d) jewellery

8. Where would you most likely find a **packing slip**?

   a) on a computer
   c) in a box that has been delivered
   b) in the garbage
   d) in the mail

9. Which of the following would not be a **seasonal** product?

   a) a coat
   c) a swimsuit
   b) a toaster
   d) candy canes

10. Which group of **variations** would you choose for a display of winter gloves?

   a) fashion, price, quality
   c) quality, sizes, comfort
   b) colours, brands, materials, sizes
   d) durability, fashion, colours

Fill in the Blanks: Monitoring Inventory

Exercise 11d

The following is a purchase order and packing slip for a shipment that your store has just received. Look at both documents and decide whether the shipment you received matches what you ordered. In the column to the right, show whether there was more (over) of a product than what was ordered or less (short) than what was ordered. If the shipment matches what was ordered, check "OK." The first three have been completed for you.

		Tina's Fashions Purchase Order		Morgan's Distribution Centre Packing Slip		Short	Over	OK
1.	20	Foxy Words Necklaces	10	Foxy Words Necklaces	10			
2.	20	Foxy Words Bracelets	13	Foxy Words Bracelets	7			
3.	20	Foxy Words Earrings	20	Foxy Words Earrings				✓
4.	6	Preston Leather Gloves-S	6	Preston Leather Gloves-S				
5.	8	Preston Leather Gloves-M	8	Preston Leather Gloves-M				
6.	6	Preston Leather Gloves-L	7	Preston Leather Gloves-L				
7.	5	Preston Wool Gloves-S	5	Preston Wool Gloves-S				
8.	5	Preston Wool Gloves-M	4	Preston Wool Gloves-M				
9.	5	Preston Wool Gloves-L	3	Preston Wool Gloves-L				
10.	30	Preston Wool Scarves	25	Preston Wool Scarves				
11.	30	Preston Silk Scarves	35	Preston Silk Scarves				
12.	9	Jake's Leather Belts-S	8	Jake's Leather Belts-S				
13.	9	Jake's Leather Belts-M	9	Jake's Leather Belts-M				
14.	7	Jake's Leather Belts-L	7	Jake's Leather Belts-L				
15.	10	Torrent Leather Belts-S	10	Torrent Leather Belts-S				
16.	20	Torrent Leather Belts-M	13	Torrent Leather Belts-M				
17.	10	Torrent Leather Belts-L	9	Torrent Leather Belts-L				
18.	9	Fancy Wool Hats-S	15	Fancy Wool Hats-S				
19.	9	Fancy Wool Hats-M	10	Fancy Wool Hats-M				
20.	18	Fancy Wool Hats-L	6	Fancy Wool Hats-L				
21.	15	Fancy Wool Socks-S	14	Fancy Wool Socks-S				
22.	15	Fancy Wool Socks-M	15	Fancy Wool Socks-M				
23.	12	Fancy Wool Socks-L	15	Fancy Wool Socks-L				
24.	12	Fancy Cotton Socks-S	12	Fancy Cotton Socks-S				
25.	12	Fancy Cotton Socks-M	8	Fancy Cotton Socks-M				
26.	8	Fancy Cotton Socks-L	12	Fancy Cotton Socks-L				

For each of the following items, indicate which season(s) or for which holiday(s) you would expect to sell the most of this merchandise.

1.	New Year's Eve		chocolate hearts
2.	St. Patrick's Day		rakes
3.	Easter		Canadian flag
4.	Halloween		flowers
5.	Hanukkah		wool hats
6.	Christmas		champagne
7.	Valentine's Day		aftershave
8.	summer		shamrocks
9.	fall		fireworks
10.	winter		chocolate eggs
11.	Mother's Day		poppies
12.	Victoria Day		menorah (candelabra)
13.	Canada Day		gardening gloves
14.	Father's Day		pumpkins
15.	Remembrance Day		turkey

Vending Machines

Read the passage and then answer the questions that follow it.

Vending machines allow customers to purchase food, drinks, and other products quickly and without long line-ups. The steps are easy. Customers simply feed the right amount of money into a **scanner** or coin slot, enter a code or pull a knob to make a selection, and wait for the machine to **release** the item into a bin at the base of the machine. If a **consumer** has not inserted enough money for his or her purchase, the machine will not release the item. The machine will also calculate and return any change that is due.

Vending machines are everywhere. They can be found in shopping malls, airports, supermarkets, arenas, cafeterias, lunchrooms, and anyplace else where people may gather. Vending machines offer people **convenience** and help save time. You can usually purchase items from vending machines outside of normal business hours. Vending machines are a great option for employees who work in out-of-the-way areas, have short lunch breaks, or work nights. Vending machines provide a way for them to buy a meal or a snack, without leaving work.

Vending machines come in different shapes and sizes depending on their location. They offer **variations** of many pre-packaged foods and drinks, including healthy food choices which follow the trend of our health-**conscious** society. Some vending machines sell non-**essential** treats such as ice cream and cookies, while others sell non-**perishable** items such as newspapers and stamps. Most public and business restrooms even have vending machines that **dispense cosmetics**, personal products, and medicines.

Although starting a business requires a lot of research and planning, vending machines can be a great investment. As your own boss, you can choose the type of machines you want, the products to sell, whether to buy or lease the machines, and where to place them. Choosing the right location is what makes a vending machine business work.

The type of products a vending machine sells can be **customized** to meet a company's needs. Products can be purchased from a **wholesale** supplier, either by visiting them in person or sending a **purchase order**. Vendors are responsible for maintaining, **monitoring, organizing,** and restocking the machines with new **inventory** on a regular basis. They must watch for **expiration** dates and must **rotate perishable** items. If the employees are happy with a vendor's products and services, the company will be too.

Comprehension Questions

Answer each question using a complete sentence.

1. How does a vending machine work?

    _____

    _____

2. What are some non-essential items that you can buy from a vending machine?

    _____

    _____

3. What are some benefits of owning vending machines?

    _____

    _____

4. How are vending machines convenient?

    _____

    _____

5. What are some non-perishable items that you can buy from a vending machine?

    _____

    _____

6. How do vending machine owners usually buy their products?

    _____

    _____

7. Why do companies like to have vending machines in their lunchrooms and break rooms?

    _____

    _____

8. Name three locations where you might find a vending machine.

    _____

    _____

Word Search:

Stocking the Shelves

```
S  E  G  R  X  D  I  S  P  E  N  S  E  X  G  O
B  O  R  G  A  N  I  Z  E  N  N  H  Y  U  I  C
E  R  R  S  U  O  I  C  S  N  O  C  C  V  V  U
T  E  A  C  H  Y  R  O  T  I  N  O  M  E  N  S
T  R  E  A  B  D  E  X  Z  J  I  N  V  E  S  T
E  M  U  N  O  P  E  L  E  Y  Z  S  I  X  I  O
S  A  V  N  E  P  P  L  K  J  H  U  M  P  N  M
G  B  S  E  A  S  O  N  A  L  E  M  G  I  V  I
C  E  S  R  E  A  C  G  A  B  X  E  D  R  E  Z
O  B  O  A  C  G  V  E  N  D  O  R  F  A  N  E
S  A  N  D  L  E  A  B  O  A  S  T  A  T  T  S
M  E  T  A  T  O  R  C  R  Y  S  V  S  I  O  S
E  N  D  P  E  R  I  S  H  A  B  L  E  O  R  E
T  W  A  R  B  D  A  E  G  R  R  A  S  N  Y  N
I  H  T  D  H  D  T  R  A  N  S  F  E  R  G  T
C  O  N  V  E  N  I  E  N  T  J  I  S  J  O  I
S  D  F  E  W  H  O  L  E  S  A  L  E  O  F  A
W  E  E  V  D  E  N  I  T  U  O  R  I  J  W  L
```

CONSCIOUS	EXPIRATION	ROUTINE
CONSUMER	INVENTORY	SCANNER
CONVENIENT	INVEST	SEASONAL
COSMETICS	MONITOR	TRANSFER
CUSTOMIZE	ORGANIZE	VARIATION
DISPENSE	PERISHABLE	VENDOR
ESSENTIAL	ROTATE	WHOLESALE

MODULE TWELVE

MERCHANDISING

VOCABULARY—Module 12

accessory	n. Something that is added to or goes with an outfit or piece of equipment that has a useful or decorative purpose; garnish, frills, extras, or trimmings, e.g., clothing accessories, bath accessories: Shoes, scarves, jewellery, and belts are all clothing *accessories*. n. A person who helps someone commit a crime, but does not take part, e.g., hiding a criminal: He was an *accessory* to murder. *also v. accessorize*
aisle	n. A long narrow space between rows of seats in a theatre, church, or airplane; a long narrow space between the rows of shelves in a large store; a passageway or walkway: You will find cosmetics in *aisle* five.
aroma	n. A strong pleasing smell; perfume, fragrance, scent, or odour: That bottle of perfume on the left has a wonderful *aroma*. *adj. aromatic*
attention	n. Notice, thought, or interest: You have my undivided *attention*. n. Watch, listen to, or think about something or someone carefully or with interest: Pay *attention* to the directions or you'll make a mistake. n. To be noticed by a lot of people: Charlie needs a lot of *attention*. n. Awareness, interest, or consideration of a particular thing or person: Many people have turned their *attention* to green energy. *adj. attentive*
attractive	adj. A good-looking, nice-looking, beautiful, gorgeous, striking, eye-catching or pretty appearance that causes interest or pleasure: There were many *attractive* people at the party. *also v. attract; adv. attractively; n. attractiveness; n. attraction*
boutique	n. A small store that sells stylish clothes, jewellery, shoes, etc.: My friend opened a designer *boutique* in Toronto.
casual	adj. Clothes that are not formal or dressy; not for special occasions; informal, relaxed, or sporty: Elizabeth wears *casual* clothes to work. adj. Not interested, indifferent, nonchalant, careless, or cavalier: His parents seem to have a very *casual* attitude about teenage drinking. adj. Not regular; temporary, unplanned, spontaneous, accidental, chance, unexpected: Bev spent her summer doing *casual* labour. *also adv. casually*

cheerful	adj. Happy, jolly, smiling, joyful, merry, positive, jovial, or lively: They are a very *cheerful* group to work with. *also adv. cheerfully; n. cheerfulness*
crowd	n. A large group of people; throng, mass, multitude, swarm, horde, mob, host, pack, assembly, gathering, group, or bunch: There was a large *crowd* lined up outside the theatre. n. A group of people who are your friends; group, set, gang, circle, or clique: Gloria's *crowd* enjoys stopping for a coffee after work. v. To put a large group of people in one place; pack, cram, pile, squeeze, or jam: They tried to *crowd* too many people into the gym. *also adj. crowded*
entice	v. Try to get someone to do something by offering them something nice; attract, tempt, lure, persuade, charm, or fascinate: Stop trying to *entice* me with chocolates. *also n. enticement; adj. enticing*
impression	n. A feeling, idea, notion, thought, intuition, or sense of what something is like: I got the *impression* that his daughter doesn't have a very good attitude. n. The way something seems, looks, or feels to a person: You will leave a bad *impression* if you are late for an interview. n. Impact, effect, influence, reaction, or sway: The lady smoking in the advertisement made a bad *impression* on my daughter. n. An imprint, dent, mark, or brand: The dental assistant took an *impression* of Angelina's teeth. n. To copy someone's speech, movements, and behaviours; imitation or impersonation: Ted did an excellent *impression* of Elvis. *also v. impress; adj. impressive*
lifestyle	n. Someone's way of life, standard of living, existence, routine, or daily life: Andrea would like to have a healthy *lifestyle*.
replenish	v. To fill something back up again; refill, stock up, top up, restock, or reload: He had to *replenish* the gas tank twice on the long trip home.
response	n. An answer, comeback, retort, rejoinder, or reaction; speaking to someone who talked to you first: George gave a funny *response* to the question. *also v. respond; adj. responsive; adv. responsively*

restrooms	n. A room with toilets in a public place, e.g., a restaurant: Part of Mel's job was to clean the public *restrooms*.
scent	n. A nice smell, fragrance, cologne, body spray, toilet water, odour, aroma, perfume, or bouquet: Those candles have a wonderful *scent*. n. On the trail of something or someone; trace: We had a little white dog named Simba who could always pick up the *scent* of chocolate. *also adj. scented*
section	n. One part of a whole; e.g., a piece of pizza, a smoking section; part, piece, segment, slice, sector, division, subdivision, fragment, portion, or bit: Restaurants no longer have smoking *sections*. v. Divide, partition, split, or segment: Could you *section* the orange for me?
spot check	n. A quick check, inspection, assessment, or examination: When Bill was working in menswear, he did many *spot checks* to make sure his area was neatly organized and there were no safety hazards.
underestimate	v. Fail to understand or guess the real cost, size, difficulty, etc., of something; i.e., underestimate a competitor; undervalue, underrate, misjudge, or miscalculate: You should never *underestimate* the power of love. *also v. estimate; n. estimation*

Finding the Meaning

Look at the word groups. Then look at the words to the right in columns A, B, C, and D. Circle the word that has the same meaning as the word group.

	WORD GROUPS	A	B	C	D
1.	goes along with something else	accessories	lifestyle	attention	create
2.	to tempt someone	impression	restrooms	entice	response
3.	stock up	replenish	response	section	entice
4.	an answer	response	replenish	cheerful	attention
5.	way of life	impression	lifestyle	cheerful	entice
6.	to have someone's interest	accessories	attention	attractive	entice
7.	joyful	impression	cheerful	entice	lifestyle
8.	a fragrance	boutique	response	cheerful	scent
9.	crowd	casual	attractive	response	group
10.	striking	entice	impression	attractive	lifestyle

The Right Word

Improve each sentence by replacing the highlighted word(s) with a word from the vocabulary list.

1. A **positive** seasonal display, a fresh **fragrance** in the air, and you as the sales associate will affect a customer's **feeling** of your store.

2. As a sales associate, you can help keep things smelling fresh in your store by cleaning displays, staying aware of **smells**, and being careful not to wear too much perfume or aftershave.

3. **Inspections** should be done frequently with particular **consideration** to **toilet areas**, product placement, traffic patterns, signs and price tags, and floors and windows.

4. First **influences** are mostly made up of sight, sound, and **smell**.

5. Certain kinds of products, such as scarves and home décor **trimmings**, sell well if they are presented in an **eye-catching** jumble.

6. "Impulse" displays, like **things that go well with other things** placed **beautifully** on or near the sales counter, **attract** customers to make additional purchases.

7. Good strategies for maintaining store displays that are **beautiful** and **happy** include, reorganizing and **replenishing** supplies and tidying products that have been mixed up by customers.

Select the correct answer.

1. Which one of the following is usually thought of as a poor **lifestyle** choice?

    a) physically active   b) family-oriented
    c) green-friendly   d) partying

2. Which product group has **expiration** dates and needs to be **replenished** often?

    a) dairy   b) jewellery
    c) stationery   d) hardware

3. In a typical North American wedding, who usually walks the bride down the **aisle**?

    a) no one   b) her mother
    c) her father   d) her husband-to-be

4. Which of the following would you most likely use to **entice** a bee?

    a) beef jerky   b) repellent spray
    c) pickled beets   d) honey

5. Which of the following is a popular **aroma** at Christmas time?

    a) pine scent   b) nutcrackers
    c) candy canes   d) stockings

6. Which of the following is the most likely to leave a poor **impression**?

    a) a festive seasonal display   b) a pushy salesperson
    c) a sanitary restroom   d) a display of colourful hats

7. People who own **casual** jackets usually wear them:

    a) everywhere   b) to work
    c) to school   d) to lunch

8. Which of the following are common bath **accessories**?

    a) hat, scarf, and gloves   b) soap, shampoo, and sponge
    c) tape measure, hammer, and nails   d) bib, bottle, and soother

9. Which activity requires the least amount of your **attention** when you are doing it?

    a) driving   b) sleeping
    c) studying   d) babysitting

10. You offer all of the customers a polite greeting as they enter the store. Which of the following would be the best **response** to your greeting?

    a) No, thank you   b) Hello
    c) Yes, please   d) I'd love to have one

Study the Words: Suffixes

A suffix is an ending that is added to a word to create a new word. The new words are similar in meaning to the original word, but they are different parts of speech.

The following words are formed by adding suffixes to the word **attract**.

		Meaning
1.	attract	v. To pull or draw someone or something towards them
2.	attractive	adj. Very pleasing in appearance or sound; causing interest or pleasure
3.	attractively	adv. Very pleasing in appearance or sound; causing interest or pleasure
4.	attraction	n. Something which makes people want to go to a place or do a particular thing
5.	attractiveness	n. Very pleasing in appearance or sound; causing interest or pleasure

Fill in the blanks below using the correct form of the word **attract**.

1. Georgina _____ men like bees to honey.

2. Nicole selected a very _____ colour scheme for the party.

3. I'm looking forward to seeing all the _____ in England and Paris.

4. Their new house is _____ decorated in a Santa Fe style.

5. Low mortgage rates have increased the _____ of owning a house.

Fill in the Blanks: Retail Store Recovery   Exercise 12e

Fill in the blanks using the words from the word bank.

WORD BANK				
aisles	enticing	restrooms	boutique	cheerful
impression	replenish	aromas	crowded	underestimate
attention	section	attractive	spot checks	accessory

Whether you work for a large department store or a small _____, store recovery is all about getting everything ready for customers. It is the combination of several processes to make the store look _____ and to simplify store operations. It should be done every day, just before either closing or opening the store. While part of store recovery can be started during store hours, it is easier and safer to complete with the doors locked. Do not _____ the importance of these tasks. Customers notice. Complete you store recovery quickly and efficiently by following these tips.

Checkout area: This is where customers will usually receive their last _____ of the store. The checkout counter should never be over-_____. It should be a _____, spacious, and inviting spot where customers can comfortably deal with their purchases. It is also where the financial transactions take place, so it should always be kept neat and orderly. _____ bag areas at the checkouts and restock any merchandise to the correct sales area. Clean doors, glass cases, _____ stands, counters, and any other visible surfaces.

Sales floor: By tidying items in our selling area, we're giving our store a neat, full appearance and deterring theft. When a shoplifter opens a package to take the contents, he/she usually throws the packaging in any empty space that is available. Filling those spaces with stock during store recovery will help to discourage shoplifters. Tidy and organize all merchandise on the sales floor. You should move all products to the front edge of the shelf or move peg hook items forward to maintain a full, _____ appearance. Collect odd pieces of merchandise in a cart and return each item to its proper location as you move from section to _____. Collect any damaged or opened packages. As well, pick up any garbage that you find as you move along. Check expiration dates on products that are perishable or consumable. Check and replace any missing tags, labels, or signs. Dust the racks, cases, and other fixtures with a clean cloth. Sweep the _____, vacuum the carpets, and mop the floor.

Stock room: Store recovery is a good time to pay _____ to the stock room. Clean work areas, empty trash cans, make sure there are no unpleasant _____, and dispose of empty boxes. Organize hangers, pricing guns, and all other store supplies. Make sure emergency exits are kept free of clutter.

Office: The office is usually out of sight from customers so it tends to be an area that gets forgotten. Plan a few minutes during the store recovery to clean the office. Secure any deposits, petty cash, or other monies. File invoices, receipts, and shipping documents along with any other paperwork for the day and create computer backups, if necessary.

Other areas for recovery: Store recovery should also include cleaning _____, the staff room, and fitting rooms. There shouldn't be any merchandise in these areas and each area should be clean. The time spent on store recovery will vary according to the size of the store and the number of employees. Keep a checklist handy and rotate tasks to make sure each area has been completed. Make _____ throughout the day. Remember, if store recovery is done regularly, maintaining the store will be manageable.

The Basics of Retail Merchandising

Read the passage and then answer the questions that follow it.

In retail, merchandising means displaying the products that are available for sale in such a way that it attracts **attention** and **entices** customers to make a purchase. Whether you are working in a small **boutique** or a large department store, there are basic rules that will help you to keep your sales up and your customers happy.

Remember that you are the one trying to **entice** the customers. They do not want to dig through piles, ask for sizes, or read advertisements in order to see what you have to offer. It has been proven, time after time, that customers will only buy what they see. The goal is to make it easy for customers to shop.

The merchandise you display in the fifteen-foot semi-circle that is visible from the store's entrance is the most important. This area is what attracts customers to your store. This is where you should place your newest and best-selling items. Keep a large inventory with variations in size, styles, and brands. **Replenish** the shelves and racks often. If a display is not kept full, customers may think that the product isn't going to be restocked and they won't even bother to look. People buying fashion items like to feel like they are discovering a new style. If the racks are starting to look empty, the customer may get the **impression** that everyone else is already wearing this item. Customers will pass by an empty-looking rack to find something newer. The same idea applies to products like electronics and cosmetics. Do frequent **spot checks** of displays to ensure that they are well-stocked and organize anything that is out of order.

When merchandising clothing, choose garment (clothing) racks that face out to display your items effectively. The right garment rack can be as important as an expensive advertisement. Front-facing merchandise always sells better than products that are hidden on the racks. Use garment racks that display clothes at the end of an **aisle** where they can be seen. People will not dig to find items in your store. They want to **casually** look around and discover things at every turn. If all the racks look the same—**crowded** and uninviting— customers won't even bother to stop and look.

Group similar items together into small, **attractive**, easy-to-shop **sections**. Place **lifestyle** items like tennis shoes and tennis rackets together. Sunglasses and similar **accessories** may be **creatively** displayed by swimwear. Keeping things together that go together is not all that hard.

For a positive **response**, especially from first-time buyers, offer special deals and discounts. They will spread the word to more people. Never **underestimate** the power of word of mouth. Be **cheerful**, polite, and kind to every customer.

Comprehension Questions

Answer each question using a complete sentence.

1. What is the purpose of merchandising products?

   _____

   _____

2. What has been proven time after time?

   _____

   _____

3. What should you never underestimate?

   _____

   _____

4. What does it mean to group items together? Give an example.

   _____

   _____

5. What might customers think if a display shelf or rack is getting empty?

   _____

   _____

6. What is the most effective way to display products?

   _____

   _____

7. Why should you do frequent spot checks of the displays?

   _____

   _____

Analogies: Analogies are links between words. You are looking for a relationship between the words. There is something similar or comparable about the words.

For example: grass is to green as sky is to blue

Directions: Complete each analogy by filling in the blank with the correct word.

WORD BANK				
injury	goggles	aroma	conceal	creative
cheerful	perishable	cosmetics	seasonal	apparel
average	population	accuse	consumer	cartons

1. tell is to reveal as hide is to _____

2. brick layer is to hard hat as welder is to _____

3. energy is to wellness as pain is to _____

4. hairdresser is to scissors as makeup artist is to_____

5. jam is to preserved as milk is to _____

6. cold is to temperature as Christmas is to _____

7. civilians are to civilization as people is to _____

8. skunk is to odour as perfume is to _____

9. sad is to happy as grumpy is to _____

10. handyman is to repairs as artist is to _____

11. home is to abode as clothing is to _____

12. visible is to unseen as unique is to _____

13. protect is to defend as blame is to _____

14. teacher is to instructor as shopper is to _____

15. barcode is to UPC as boxes are to _____

Review 3: Antonyms
Modules 9–12

Directions: Match the words in Column A with the words in Column B that have an opposite meaning.

	COLUMN A	COLUMN B
1.	confront	release
2.	attractive	safe
3.	promptly	unnecessary
4.	organize	avoid
5.	detain	daydreaming
6.	attention	concealed
7.	expensive	depressed
8.	replenish	late
9.	hazardous	ugly
10.	visible	cheap
11.	essential	mess up
12.	cheerful	reduce

Review 3: Suffixes
Modules 9–12

Which word is not correct? Circle the word with the incorrect suffix.

1. accessory	accessorize	accessorying
2. attention	attentivement	attentive
3. entice	enticely	enticement
4. impress	impressive	impressly
5. invest	investering	investment
6. convenient	convenience	convenientive
7. conscious	consciousment	consciousness
8. protect	protectiveness	protectment
9. visible	visibility	visibleness
10. operate	operational	operativeness
11. coordinate	coordination	coordinatively
12. dispense	despensive	dispensable

A suffix is an ending that is added to a word to create a new word. The new words are similar in meaning to the original word, but they are different parts of speech.

Meaning

1. vary

v. To change or cause something to change in amount or level, especially from one occasion to another

2. various

adj. Many different

3. variation

n. A change in amount or level
n. Something that is slightly different from the usual form or arrangement

4. variable

n. A number, amount, or situation which can change

5. variable

adj. Likely to change often

6. variability

n. The quality, state, or degree of being variable or changeable.

Fill in the blanks below using the correct form of the word **vary**.

1. Samantha found the conversation about genetic _____ very confusing.

2. The new houses in our neighbourhood _____ in size from 1500 square feet to 2600 square feet.

3. His study ignored important _____(s) like credit rating, job history, savings, and marital status.

4. The ice cream shop sells _____ flavours of ice cream.

5. The bank offers _____ interest rates on that account.

6. There was very little _____ in the temperature this past week.

274 VOCABULARY WORDS

* The bracketed numbers indicate the module where the vocabulary word is introduced.

abusive – (3)
accessible – (2)
accessory – (12)
accommodate – (2)
accomplish – (6)
account – (9)
accurate – (8)
accuse – (9)
acknowledge – (7)
addition – (4)
additional – (7)
administrative – (9)
admission – (2)
advertise – (6)
affect – (10)
affordable – (5)
aisle – (12)
alert – (10)
alternative – (3)
apologize – (3)
apparel – (9)
appointment – (4)
appreciate – (6)
approach – (3)
appropriate – (2)
aroma – (12)
arrest – (9)
assembly – (5)
assign – (10)
assist – (4)
assume – (6)
atmosphere – (2)
attention – (12)
attitude – (3)
attract – (3)
attractive – (12)
authorization – (8)
available – (3)
average – (9)
awkward – (10)
bar code – (8)
barrier – (10)
benefit – (5)
boutique – (12)
brand – (5)
calculate – (8)
cartons – (10)
casual – (12)
challenge – (4)
change – (8)
check – (8)
cheerful – (12)
cheque – (8)
classic – (5)
clearance – (6)

close – (7)
code – (8)
collect – (7)
combination – (8)
comment – (7)
commission – (8)
commit – (8)
communicate – (2)
compare – (1)
competitor – (6)
complaint – (3)
compliment – (1)
complimentary – (2)
conceal – (9)
concern – (10)
condition – (5)
confirm – (4)
confront – (9)
conscious – (11)
consistent – (8)
consumer – (11)
contact – (4)
contest – (6)
contract – (1)
convenient – (11)
coordinate – (10)
correct – (5)
cosmetics – (11)
coupon – (6)
courteous – (1)
co-workers – (10)
create – (1)
credit – (7)
crowd – (12)
customer – (1)
customize – (11)
decision – (2)
defective – (3)
demonstrate – (5)
detain – (9)
deter – (9)
dimensions – (5)
disability – (2)
disappoint – (2)
disclose – (7)
discount – (3)
discretion – (7)
dispense – (11)
display – (1)
effective – (6)
encourage – (4)
enhance – (4)
ensure – (4)
entice – (12)
error – (9)

essential – (11)
estimate – (2)
examine – (9)
example – (6)
exception – (7)
exchange – (7)
exist – (3)
expensive – (9)
experience – (2)
expiration – (11)
facility – (2)
famous – (5)
features – (5)
feedback – (2)
follow-up – (4)
fragile – (8)
fraud – (7)
garment – (6)
goggles – (10)
greet – (1)
handle – (7)
hazardous – (10)
identical – (8)
identification – (8)
image – (1)
impress – (1)
impression – (12)
incentive – (6)
indicate – (7)
includes – (5)
income – (10)
inconvenience – (3)
increase – (2)
influence – (2)
information – (1)
injury – (10)
inspect – (10)
instruct – (5)
interests – (4)
internal – (9)
inventory – (11)
invest – (11)
key – (7)
knowledge – (1)
label – (5)
lifestyle – (12)
limit – (7)
listen – (1)
loyal – (1)
mannequin – (6)
manufacturer – (3)
merchandise – (3)
message – (4)
modify – (7)
monitor – (11)

neutral – (5)
objection – (5)
occupation – (10)
offer – (4)
operate – (10)
opportunity – (4)
option – (5)
organization – (2)
organize – (11)
original – (7)
outcome – (8)
outfit – (6)
overloaded – (10)
packing slip – (11)
participate – (8)
perishable – (11)
permanent – (5)
personal – (1)
personality – (1)
personalize – (2)
policy – (1)
popular – (5)
population – (9)
POS terminals – (8)
positive – (1)
possess – (5)
preference – (4)
prevent – (7)
procedure – (8)
product – (1)
professional – (1)
profit – (6)
program – (4)
promotion – (6)
promptly – (9)
protect – (10)
purchase order – (11)
quality – (3)
rack – (6)
rebate – (6)
receipt – (8)
recommend – (2)
reconcile – (8)
records – (4)
refund – (7)
relate – (6)
relationship – (1)
replenish – (12)
require – (7)
research – (3)
resolve – (3)
resources – (2)
response – (12)
restrooms – (12)
review – (7)

responsibility – (8)
role – (7)
rotate – (11)
routine – (11)
sale – (1)
sales associate – (2)
safety – (10)
satisfy – (1)
scanner – (11)
scent – (12)
schedule – (4)
seasonal – (11)
section – (12)
security – (9)
select – (4)
sense – (2)
shelf – (10)
shift – (8)
shipment – (5)
shoplifting – (8)
shrinkage – (9)
signal – (7)
solution – (3)
spot checks – (12)
status – (5)
stepladder – (10)
stock – (5)
strategy – (6)
success – (3)
suggest – (6)
survey – (9)
suspect – (9)
target – (9)
technique – (7)
theft – (9)
train – (2)
transfer – (11)
trend – (6)
uncertain – (7)
underestimate – (12)
unique – (2)
UPC – (11)
upcoming – (4)
update – (4)
upgrade – (6)
valuable – (6)
variation – (11)
vendor – (11)
verify – (8)
visible – (10)
volume – (5)
voluntary – (8)
warranty – (3)
wholesale – (11)
witness – (9)

ANSWER KEY: MODULE 1

a.	b.	c.	d.	e.
1. a	1. greet, customers	1. c	1. common	1. production
2. c	2. professional, personality, customer	2. c	2. complete	2. creation
3. d	3. create, relationship, creating, loyal	3. b	3. conduct	3. information
4. b	4. courteous, listen, customer's, information, customer	4. c	4. political	4. impression
5. a	5. relationships, loyalty	5. d	5. break	5. relation
6. b	6. compliment, positive, policy	6. a	6. partner	6. contraction
7. a	7. create, image, knowledge, products, display	7. b	7. discipline	7. position
8. d	8. personality, sales	8. c	8. quest	8. satisfaction
9. d	9. customer, satisfy, personal, customers	9. c	9. present	
10. c		10. c	10. informal	
11. c			11. listen	
12. a			12. careful	
			13. leader	
			14. public	
			15. chosen	
			16. position	
			17. policy	
			18. graceful	
			19. protect	
			20. current	
			21. sail	
			22. personal	
			23. great	

f.

customer, impression
greeting
positive, professional, create, loyal, relationship
listen, courteous
personally
products, knowledge
display
sales

g.

1. The customer bought a new cell phone at the store today.
2. The customer was impressed by the interactive displays, the large selection of products, and the courteous manner of Tom, the assistant sales manager.
3. When the customer came into the store, Tom was serving another customer.
4. The customer was even happier about his purchase because the phone he chose was on sale.
5. Tom found out what kind of phone the customer needed by asking questions and listening carefully.
6. If the store doesn't have the product the customer is looking for, you could direct them to a store that does have the product.
7. Tom's job title is assistant sales manager.
8. What do you use your phone for: business, personal, or both? How often do you use your phone? What features are most important to you? (various answers)

ANSWER KEY: MODULE 2

a.	b.	c.	d.	e.	f.
1. c 2. b 3. d 4. a 5. a 6. b 7. a 8. b 9. b 10. a	1. sales associate, influence, decision, experience 2. accommodate 3. resources 4. unique 5. accommodate, disabilities, experience 6. appropriate 7. accessible, trained, accessible 8. organizations, admission, facilities 9. feedback, increase, estimated	1. d 2. b 3. c 4. d 5. c 6. d 7. b 8. c 9. b	1. inexperience 2. inappropriate 3. inaccessible 4. indecision 5. inability	1. A 13. S 2. S 14. S 3. S 15. A 4. A 16. S 5. S 17. S 6. S 18. A 7. S 19. A 8. S 20. S 9. A 21. S 10. A 22. S 11. S 23. S 12. S 24. A	1. feedback, facility 2. sales associate 3. accessible, disabilities 4. accommodated 5. admission 6. trained 7. appropriately 8. complimentary 9. atmosphere 10. estimate 11. recommend 12. experience 13. facility

g.
1. The name of the new standard is: Accessible Customer Service Standard.
2. Nearly 1.85 million people in Ontario have disabilities.
3. An assistive device is a tool that helps people with disabilities to perform daily activities, e.g., a cane, dog, glasses, hearing aid.
4. It is estimated that customers with disabilities spend $25 billion every year.
5. A support person may help someone with a disability to try on clothes in a change room or help them to use the restroom.
6. The new standard comes into effect on January 1, 2012.
7. The number of people with disabilities is growing because the number of people over the age of 65 who have disabilities is increasing.
8. Accessible customer service makes good business sense because people with disabilities spend a lot of money on goods and services.

h.

```
S S R E S O U R C E S R A B C D
U N I Q U E V N B M K E P E E K
A D M I S S I O N N B C P F Y M
A Y D W P T R A I N O O R G T Y
C N E G I I Q A N J L M O D I O
C L C E H M U E F F L M P S L R
O D I X G A E F L F J E R R I G
M R S C F T B G U D H N I G B A
M T I B D E C A E W G D A D A N
O Y O C O M M U N I C A T E S I
D H N C U M N B C E R T E T I Z
A J T E T R F E E D B A C K D A
T A C C E S S I B L E K M H F T
E R E H P S O M T A I I H W F I
X C O M P L I M E N T A R Y J O
S C D G E C N E I R E P X E U N
```

162

ANSWER KEY: MODULE 3

a.	b.	c.	d.	e.	
1. b 2. c 3. d 4. b 5. d 6. b 7. c 8. a 9. d 10. a 11. b	1. warranty, quality 2. merchandise 3. successful, attitude, existing, approach 4. alternatives, discount 5. complaints 6. abusive 7. attract 8. resolved 9. attracting, existing	1. c 2. c 3. a 4. a 5. b 6. b 7. b 8. d 9. b 10. c	1. unsuccessful 2. unavailable 3. unresolved 4. unapproachable 5. unattractive	1. approached 2. quality 3. research 4. manufacturer 5. defective 6. inconvenient 7. existing	8. alternative 9. merchandise 10. resolve 11. available 12. solution 13. complaint

f.

1. You should treat a customer who is returning an item with the same courtesy and respect you would show a customer who is purchasing something new.
2. The six steps to follow when handling a customer complaint are: (1) Make sure that you thank the customer for bringing the problem to your attention. (2) Listen carefully to make sure you understand the problem. (3) Apologize for any inconvenience the customer has experienced. (4) Ask for any extra information you may need to help resolve the problem. (5) Offer a solution to the problem. (6) Solve the problem or find someone who can.
3. A return policy is a set of rules that have been created by a company that explain if and how a product can be returned to the store for an exchange or refund.
4. Customer feedback is the information and opinions that a customer gives you about their experience with your company's products and services.
5. The way that a company treats its existing customers helps it to keep existing customers and attract new customers. This sets a company apart from its competitors.
6. Having the right attitude and approach to handling complaints will make your job more satisfying and improve your customer service skills.

g.

1. alternatives 2. complaints 3. discounts 4. manufacturers 5. solutions	6. warranties 7. defects 8. apologies 9. successes

ANSWER KEY: MODULE 4

a.	b.		c.	d.	e.	
1. c	1. interests, preferences	5. preference, encourage, ensure	1. b	1. reschedule	1. interesting	9. follow up
2. a	2. schedule, contact	6. follow-up, opportunity, ensure, offer, upcoming	2. c	2. reprogram	2. select	10. offer
3. a	3. preferences	7. records, interests	3. c	3. reconfirm	3. encourage	11. appointments
4. a	4. schedule, confirm, appointment, message		4. c	4. reselect	4. messages	12. upcoming
5. b			5. d		5. contact	13. program
6. b			6. c		6. ensuring	14. challenging
7. d			7. b		7. addition	15. preference
8. a			8. d		8. enhance	
9. c			9. b			
10. b			10. b			

f.

1. It would have made the letter more personal if the store had used the customers' names in the letter they sent out.
2. The store is enhancing its services by offering customers appointments with personal shoppers.
3. The new service is complimentary (free).
4. If you are not home when the store contacts you about their new service, the caller will leave a voice mail or contact you by e-mail.
5. The sales associates at this store know what their customers like because they keep records of their customers' purchases and preferences.
6. The store will give you a follow-up call to ensure that you were satisfied with your shopping experience.
7. If you would like to try their new service right away, you should give the store a call.
8. The store does a follow-up with customers to make sure that they are satisfied with the products and services they have received from the store.

ANSWER KEY: REVIEW 1

a.	b.	c.
1. courteous	1. courteous, professional	1. negative -9
2. disappointing	2. compliment my hair, solution to my problem, discount on my next purchase	2. rude - 5
3. complimentary	3. apologize, accommodate disabilities, follow up with customers	3. gentle - 6
4. customers	4. schedule an appointment, take a message, call the manufacturer	4. expensive - 3
5. influence	5. has a very positive image, has many loyal customers	5. ignore - 1
6. communicate	6. explain our return policy	6. problem - 8
7. alternative	7. offered some positive feedback	7. busy - 12
8. personal	8. give them our decision, update the return policy	8. public - 2
9. apologize		9. disappointed - 4
10. listen		10. unfaithful - 7
11. abusive		11. common - 11
12. unique		12. perfect - 10
13. feedback		13. decrease - 14
14. defective		14. failure – 13
15. loyal		15. destroy – 15

ANSWER KEY: MODULE 5

a.	b.	c.	d.		e.
1. a	1. instructions, assembly	1. c	1. loss	13. approval	1. include
2. c	2. permanent, labels, include	2. b	2. unique	14. benefits	2. classic
3. b	3. features	3. a	3. wrong	15. expensive	3. assemble
4. d	4. features, benefits	4. b	4. unknown	16. correction	4. popular
5. a	5. feature, benefit	5. d	5. hide	17. style	5. features
6. b	6. objections, objection	6. b	6. favourite	18. brandy	6. benefit
7. d	7. possess, status, classic, neutral, affordable, brand	7. b	7. class	19. excludes	7. feature
8. c	8. famous, demonstrate, features, benefits, popular, demonstrations, assembly, options, stock	8. b	8. type	20. prejudice	8. options
9. a		9. b	9. powerless	21. feature	9. dimensions
10. d		10. b	10. temporary	22. learn	10. include
11. b			11. hated	23. meeting	11. neutral
			12. optimal		12. brands
					13. stock
					14. shipments
					15. permanent

f.	g.	
1. c, d, a, e, b	1. accomplishments	6. strategies
2. d, e, a, c, b	2. competitors	7. trends
3. c, d, a, b, e	3. contests	8. upgrades
	4. coupons	9. rebates
	5. examples	10. promotions

ANSWER KEY: MODULE 6

a.	b.		c.	d.	e.
1. a	1. trends,	6. example,	1. c	1. accomplishment	1. false
2. b	effective,	strategy,	2. c	2. uncontested	2. true
3. a	appreciate	rebates	3. d	3. unassuming	3. false
4. c	2. promotes,	7. incentive	4. a	4. unrelated	4. false
5. b	trends	8. assumed,	5. b	5. effectiveness	5. true
6. d	3. advertised	trend,	6. c	6. unappreciative	6. true
7. a	4. contests	profits,	7. d	7. advertisement	7. false
8. c	5. promotions,	valuable,	8. a		8. true
9. d	promotions,	upgrade	9. b		9. true
10. b	competitors				10. false
					11. false
					12. true

f.

1. Suggestive selling means suggesting to customers that they might like to also purchase another item(s) to go with the item(s) they have already decided to purchase.
2. Customers expect suggestive selling because some products are not complete without additional items that need to be purchased separately. For example, a customer would be upset if he/she bought a toy and then got home to find that the item requires batteries and the sales associate hadn't said anything. It would mean he/she would have to go back out to buy batteries. Suggestive selling helps to make sure that customers are completely satisfied with their product(s) and the service they received.
3. Suggestive selling can be used with online shopping by having pop-up windows to show complimentary items (items that match or are related to) the item(s) being considered or purchased. For example, showing books by the same author or a hat that matches a scarf and gloves.
4. You can use suggestive selling without saying anything at all by having a garment rack or mannequin displaying accessories, batteries, or other related products near the checkout.
5. It is important for sales associates to care about whether or not they sell the store's products because if they don't sell anything, the store owners won't make enough money to pay their bills and, most importantly, they won't have enough money to pay their employees.

g.

1.	accomplishments	6.	strategies
2.	competitors	7.	trends
3.	contests	8.	upgrades
4.	coupons	9.	rebates
5.	examples	10.	promotions

ANSWER KEY: MODULE 7

a.	b.	c.		d.	e.
1. a	1. key	1. d	1. S	14. A	1. collective
2. c	2. closed	2. b	2. S	15. S	2. collector
3. a	3. comment, indicate	3. a	3. A	16. S	3. collectable
4. d	4. uncertain, collect	4. c	4. S	17. A	4. collect
5. c	5. exchange, uncertain	5. d	5. S	18. S	5. collection
6. b	6. additional	6. d	6. A	19. S	6. collectively
7. d	7. comment, indicate	7. b	7. A	20. S	
8. a	8. discretion, refunds	8. d	8. S	21. S	
9. b		9. b	9. S	22. S	
10. b			10. S	23. S	
			11. S	24. S	
			12. S	25. A	
			13. S		

f.

1. The four conditions for returning or exchanging a product are: (a) it must be returned within 90 days, (b) in its original condition, (c) in its original packaging, and (d) with your receipt.
2. If you don't have your receipt, a return will be made at the discretion of the manager on duty at the time.
3. Three products that are exceptions to the policy are electronics which must be returned within thirty days, and ink and DVDs, which may be returned if unopened. (also media, memory cards, books, CDs, mattresses, portable bed)
4. Three products that are not refundable are paint, magazines, and fireworks. (also stain, products cut to length or modified, clearance, or final sale merchandise)
5. The refund policy for shipping charges is that they can only be refunded on gift cards if there was an error on the part of the store.
6. The refund and return policy for gift cards is that they are neither returnable nor refundable.
7. The personal information that the store asks you for is your name, home address, phone number, and valid identification.

g.

Across
2. credit
5. disclose
7. comment
9. technique
10. refund
11. key

Down
1. fraud
2. closed
3. discretion
4. collect
6. exchange
8. modify

ANSWER KEY: MODULE 8

a.	b.	c.	d.	e.
1. b	1. combination, change	1. b	1. authorization	1. check
2. b	2. procedures, shift, POS terminal	2. a	2. participate	2. responsibility, shift, cheque
3. c	3. identification, cheque, verify, cheque	3. d	3. commission	3. participate, combination, fragile
4. b	4. cheque, responsibility, check, cheque, identification	4. b	4. check	4. procedures, POS terminal, verifying identification, authorization, change, receipt
5. a	5. authorization	5. d	5. identical	
6. c	6. POS terminals	6. c	6. calculate	
7. d	7. calculating, commissions, identification	7. b	7. responsibility	5. outcome
8. a		8. b	8. commit	
9. c		9. d	9. identification	
10. b		10. b	10. cheque	
			11. combination	
			12. accurate	

f.

1. The Scanner Price Accuracy Voluntary Code was developed by the Retail Council of Canada, the Canadian Association of Chain Drug Stores, the Canadian Federation of Independent Grocers, and the Canadian Council of Grocery Distributors.
2. The code was put into place in June 2002.
3. According to the Scanner Price Accuracy Code, you will receive the first bag for free because it is less than $10 and the second bag will be rung in at the scanned price of $8.99.
4. A participating store will have the Scanner Price Accuracy Voluntary Code posted by the store entrance or checkout.
5. If you are not satisfied with a cashier's refusal to honour the code, you may speak to the store manager or supervisor. If you are still not satisfied, you may register a complaint with the Scanner Price Accuracy Committee.
6. According to the Scanner Price Accuracy Code, you will pay $10.99 for both as they are part of an advertised price. You will not receive one item for free because the price of the item is more than $10.00.

ANSWER KEY: REVIEW 2

a.	b.	c.	d.
1. contest	1. other shoe stores, department stores that sell shoes	5. Loretta demonstrating, the combination of the safe	1. technique	1. correctly
2. competition			2. additional	2. accomplishment
3. fraud		6. on the new product line	3. clearance	3. permanently
4. key	2. on weekends only, after 5:00 p.m. on Saturdays	7. at the manager's discretion	4. uncertain	4. acknowledgement
5. cheque			5. advertise	5. additionally
6. commission		8. Mark's commission, the total of today's receipts	6. require	6. closely
7. fragile	3. ended on Friday		7. coupons	7. requirement
8. close	4. verify that information, show you an example, exchange this ring, see some identification		8. signal	8. effectively
9. prevent			9. discretion	9. advertisement
10. promotion			10. acknowledge	10. commitment
			11. opportunity	11. neutrally
			12. competitor	

e.

1. incorrect	5. anonymous	9. tough
2. different	6. different	10. inconsistent
3. wrong	7. involuntary	11. less
4. separate	8. biased	12. prevent

ANSWER KEY: MODULE 9

a.	b.	c.	d.	e.
1. a	1. expensive	1. a	1. administer	1. shrinkage
2. b	2. suspect, conceal, witnessed, theft, accuse	2. b	2. administrator	2. deter
3. a	3. shrinkage	3. c	3. administrative	3. theft
4. a	4. theft, conceals	4. c	4. administration	4. examine
5. d	5. accusing, detain, suspect	5. b	5. administer	5. promptly
6. c	6. confront, detain, witness, concealing	6. b	6. administration	6. apparel
7. b	7. security, shrinkage, theft	7. b		7. security
8. a		8. a		8. concealed
9. d		9. d		9. expensive
10. c		10. b		10. security
				11. administrative
				12. errors
				13. survey
				14. suspect
				15. witnessed

f.

1. Shrinkage is the loss that a business suffers due to shoplifting, employee theft, employee errors, and vendor/manufacturer/distributor fraud (overcharging retailers/shorting orders).
2. The statistics from the passage come from the 2010 Global Retail Theft Barometer that was produced by the Centre for Retail Research.
3. The number one cause of shrinkage is shoplifting. It cost retailers $45.5 billion.
4. Two high-shrink items are accessories and children's wear.
5. Vendor fraud is when vendors charges too much for merchandise or don't give the retailer as many items in the package as what they have charged for.
6. The countries that have the lowest shrink rates are Austria, Hong Kong, and Taiwan.
7. Forty-two countries participated in the survey.
8. The second-largest cause of shrinkage is employee theft. It cost Retailers $37.8 billion.

ANSWER KEY: MODULE 10

a.	b.	c.	d.		e.
1. d	1. hazardous, shelf, overloaded	1. d	1. effects	1. inspect	10. awkward
2. b		2. b	2. effects	2. safety	11. operators
3. a	2. income	3. a	3. effect	3. concern	12. inspected
4. d	3. barrier	4. c	4. affect	4. barriers	13. visible
5. c	4. stepladder	5. d	5. effect	5. cartons	14. injury
6. b	5. cartons, barrier, alert	6. b	6. affect	6. stepladders	15. hazardous
7. b		7. d	7. effects	7. barriers	16. protected
8. d	6. safety, hazardous	8. b	8. affected	8. shelves	17. co-worker
9. d	7. awkward, safety, concerns, co-workers	9. c	9. affect	9. overloaded	18. goggles
10. a		10. b	10. affected		

f.

1. false	4. true	7. true
2. false	5. false	8. false
3. true	6. true	9. false
		10. true

g.

Across	Down	
1. visible	2. injury	6. barrier
8. cartons	3. awkward	7. goggles
11. coordinate	4. income	9. occupation
12. affect	5. inspect	10. hazardous
14. alert		12. assign
		13. shelf

ANSWER KEY: MODULE 11

a.	b.	c.	d.	e.

a.
1. b
2. c
3. a
4. a
5. b
6. b
7. a
8. c
9. b
10. b

b.
1. monitoring, inventory, essential
2. inventory, transferred, vendor
3. perishable, essential, expiration
4. purchase order
5. packing slip
6. organized, cosmetics, variations
7. vendor, scanner, inventory, seasonal

c.
1. c
2. a
3. b
4. b
5. b
6. a
7. d
8. c
9. b
10. b

d.
1. -10
2. -10
3. OK
4. OK
5. OK
6. +1
7. OK
8. -1
9. +2
10. -5
11. +5
12. +1
13. OK
14. OK
15. OK
16. -7
17. -1
18. +6
19. +1
20. -12
21. -1
22. OK
23. +3
24. OK
25. -4
26. +4

e.
1. champagne
2. shamrocks
3. chocolate eggs
4. pumpkins
5. menorah
6. turkey
7. chocolate hearts
8. gardening gloves
9. rakes
10. wool hats
11. flowers
12. fireworks
13. Canadian flag
14. aftershave
15. poppies

f.
1. A vending machine sells items for set prices. You put your money into the slot and then select the item you want. The machine will release the item and give you any change that is due.
2. Some non-essential items that you can buy from a vending machine include ice cream and cookies.
3. Some benefits of owning a vending machine are: (1) you can buy or rent a vending machine, (2) you can put them in as many places as you like, (3) you can customize a machine to meet a company's needs.
4. Vending machines are convenient because they can fit in all different locations, they can be "open for business" 24/7, and if they are in a company lunchroom the staff can avoid going out for meals.
5. Some non-perishable items that you can buy from a vending machine include newspapers, stamps, cosmetics, personal products, and medicines.
6. Vending machine owners usually buy their products from a wholesale supplier.
7. Companies like to have vending machines in their lunchrooms and break rooms because it keeps their staff happy and they can take care of business without having to worry about the day–to-day operations of a vending machine. If a company has staff working 24/7 shifts, the staff will have access to vending machines products outside of regular business hours.
8. Vending machines can be found in shopping malls, airports, supermarkets, arenas, cafeterias, lunchrooms, and anyplace else where people may gather.

g.

S	E	G	R	X	D	I	S	P	E	N	S	E	X	G	O
B	O	R	G	A	N	I	Z	E	N	N	H	Y	U	I	C
E	R	R	S	U	O	I	C	S	N	O	C	C	V	V	U
T	E	A	C	H	Y	R	O	T	I	N	O	M	E	N	S
T	R	E	A	B	D	E	X	Z	J	I	N	V	E	S	T
E	M	U	N	O	P	E	L	E	Y	Z	S	I	X	I	O
S	A	V	N	E	P	P	L	K	J	H	U	M	P	N	M
G	B	S	E	A	S	O	N	A	L	E	M	G	I	V	I
C	E	S	R	E	A	C	G	A	B	X	E	D	R	E	Z
O	B	O	A	C	G	V	E	N	D	O	R	F	A	N	E
S	A	N	D	L	E	A	B	O	A	S	T	A	T	T	S
M	E	T	A	T	O	R	C	R	Y	S	V	S	I	O	S
E	N	D	P	E	R	I	S	H	A	B	L	E	O	R	E
T	W	A	R	B	D	A	E	G	R	R	A	S	N	Y	N
I	H	T	D	H	D	T	R	A	N	S	F	E	R	G	T
C	O	N	V	E	N	I	E	N	T	J	I	S	J	O	I
S	D	F	E	W	H	O	L	E	S	A	L	E	O	F	A
W	E	E	V	D	E	N	I	T	U	O	R	I	J	W	L

ANSWER KEY: MODULE 12

a.	b.		c.	d.	e.	
1. a	1. cheerful, scent, impression	5. accessories, attractive	1. d	1. attracts	1. boutique	9. enticing
2. c		6. accessories, attractively, entice	2. a	2. attractive	2. attractive	10. section
3. a	2. aromas		3. c	3. attractions	3. underestimate	11. aisles
4. a	3. spot checks, attention, restrooms	7. attractive, cheerful, replenishing	4. d	4. attractively	4. impression	12. attention
5. b			5. a	5. attractiveness	5. crowded	13. aromas
6. b			6. b		6. cheerful	14. restrooms
7. b	4. impressions, scent		7. a		7. replenish	15. spot checks
8. d			8. b		8. accessory	
9. d			9. b			
10. c			10. b			

f.

1. The purpose of merchandising products is to attract attention and entice customers to make a purchase.
2. It has been proven time after time that customers will only buy what they see.
3. You should never underestimate the power of word of mouth.
4. Grouping items together means putting things together that belong together. For example, hat, gloves, and scarves go together; earrings and necklaces go together; shirts and ties go together.
5. If a display shelf or rack is getting empty, customers may think that everyone is already wearing the item and pass it by. They may also think that the product isn't going to be restocked, so they won't even bother to look.
6. The most effective way to display products is front-facing at the end of an aisle.
7. You should do frequent spot checks of displays to ensure that they are well-stocked and to organize anything that is out of order.

ANSWER KEY: REVIEW 3

a.	b.	c.	d.
1. conceal	1. avoid	1. accessorize	1. variability
2. goggles	2. ugly	2. attentive	2. vary
3. injury	3. late	3. enticement	3. variables
4. cosmetics	4. mess up	4. impressive	4. various
5. perishable	5. release	5. investment	5. variable
6. seasonal	6. daydreaming	6. convenience	6. variation
7. population	7. cheap	7. consciousness	
8. aroma	8. reduce	8. protectiveness	
9. cheerful	9. safe	9. visibility	
10. creative	10. concealed	10. operational	
11. apparel	11. unnecessary	11. coordination	
12. average	12. depressed	12. dispensable	
13. accuse			
14. consumer			
15. cartons			

References

"Accessible Customer Service Standards." Ontario Ministry of Community and Social Services. http://www.mcss.gov.on.ca/en/mcss/programs/accessibility/ComplyingStandards/customerService/index.aspx

"Accessible Customer Service." July 31, 2007. Ontario Government, Service Ontario e-Laws. http://www.e-laws.gov.on.ca/html/source/regs/english/2007/elaws_src_regs_r07429_e.htm

Berman, Rob. "Marketing Lagniappe: Do You Have It?" 1 Feb. 2011. EzineArticles.com. http://ezinearticles.com/?Marketing-Lagniappe:-Do-You-Have-It?&id=5837925

Broadus, Lola. "Providing More than Expected: Lagniappe." 22 Jun. 2007 EzineArticles.com. http://ezinearticles.com/?Providing-More-than-Expected—Lagniappe&id=616919

"Cambridge Learner's Dictionary." Cambridge Dictionaries Online. 2004. Cambridge University Press. Cambridge Dictionaries Online - Cambridge University Press.htm>.http://dictionaries.cambridge.org

Cooperberg, Chaya. "Skip the Extended Warranty this Season." November 27, 2009. *The Globe and Mail*. http://www.theglobeandmail.com/globe-investor/personal-finance/home-cents/skip-the-extended-warranty-this-season/article1379843/

Cosgrove, Dan. "The Key to Suggestive Selling is 'Repeat.'" mercsystems.com. http://www.mercsystems.com/article_thekeytosuggestiveselling.php

Crisp Publications Inc. Retailing Smarts Series, workbook edition. Axzo Press, 2006.

Dictionary.com Unabridged. Random House, Inc. 30 Mar. 2011. <Dictionary.com http://dictionary.reference.com

"Extended Warranties." Consumer Challenges and Solutions, Canadian Consumer Information Gateway; Reproduced with the permission of the Minister of Public Works and Government Services, 2011; http://consumerinformation.ca/app/oca/ccig/consumerChallenge.do?consumerChallengeNo=942&language=eng

"Extended Warranties." The Better Business Bureau. http://www.bbb.org/canada/SitePage.aspx?site=162&id=44452fb3-54c7-495b-a5ab-354c75d10aeb

Fitzgerald, Nancy. "Turning Christmas Tree History Upside Down." 9 Jun. 2006. EzineArticles.com. http://ezinearticles.com/?Turning-Christmas-Tree-History-Upside-Down&id=216597

Garvey, John P. "Retail Clothing Merchandising Basics." 14 Jul. 2009 EzineArticles.com. http://ezinearticles.com/?Retail-Clothing-Merchandising-Basics&id=2608418

Garvey, John P. "Suggestive Selling." 27 Jul. 2010 EzineArticles.com. http://ezinearticles.com/?Suggestive-Selling&id=4747861

"The Global Theft Barometer 2010." September 28, 2010. The Centre for Retail Research http://www.retailresearch.org/grtb_globaltrends.php

Klein, Karen. "Build Customer Relations by Listening." June 1, 2007. Businessweek.com. http://www.businessweek.com/smallbiz/content/jun2007/sb20070601_858776.htm

Lyter, Laura. "Upside Down Christmas Tree: Features, Benefits, and Options of This Holiday Decor." 5 Oct. 2010. *EzineArticles.com.* http://ezinearticles.com/?Upside-Down-Christmas-Tree—Features,--Benefits,-and-Options-of-This-Holiday-Decor&id=5151624

Maier, Ron B. "The Basics of Merchandising." 25 Nov. 2008. EzineArticles.com. http://ezinearticles.com/?The-Basics-of-Merchandising&id=1729885

Mathias, Kevin. "Starting a Vending Machine Business." March 15, 2011. Buzzle.com. http://www.buzzle.com/articles/starting-vending-machine-business.html

Merriam-Webster Online Dictionary. 2008. Merriam-Webster Online. http://www.merriam-webster.com/dictionary/

Miller, Cash Justin. "How to Build Customer Relationships." November 6, 2008. Suite101.com http://www.suite101.com/content/how-to-build-customer-relationships-a77101

Miller, Michelle. "5 Ways to Rock Her Experience at the Cash Register." August 24, 2009. http://www.marketingshebang.com/2009/08/5-ways-to-rock-her-experience-at-the-cash-register/.

"Retail Theft Prevention Tips". March, 25, 2011. http://diogenesllc.com/retailtheftprevention.pdf

Richardson, Melvin. "Why Are Vending Machines Good?" ehow.com. http://www.ehow.com/about_5314279_vending-machines-good.html

"Safety is Everyone's Business." July 24, 2006. Work Safe BC. http://www.worksafebc.com/publications/health_and_safety/by_topic/assets/pdf/safetyonthejob.pdf

Say, Rosa. "The Six Basic Needs of Customers." April 27, 2010 lifehack.org. http://www.lifehack.org/articles/management/the-six-basic-needs-of-customers.html

"Scanner Price Accuracy Voluntary Code." May 29, 2002. Competition Bureau Canada; Reproduced with the permission of the Minister of Public Works and Government Services, 2011; http://www.competitionbureau.gc.ca/eic/site/cb-bc.nsf/vwapj/ct02380e.pdf/$file/ct02380e.pdf

"Scanner Price Accuracy Voluntary Code." Retail Council of Canada. http://www.retailcouncil.org/advocacy/national/issues/cp/scanner_accuracy02_eng.asp

Stucker, Cathy. "Do You Want Fries With That?: Using Suggestive Selling to Increase Your Sales." 27 Mar. 2005. EzineArticles.com. http://ezinearticles.com/?Do-You-Want-Fries-With-That?—Using-Suggestive-Selling-to-Increase--Your-Sales&id=23709

Tahir, Liz. "Customer Service That Will Keep Them Coming Back." about.com. http://sbinfocanada.about.com/od/customerservice/a/custservtipslt.htm

Waters, Shari. "Retail Store Recovery: How to Ready Your Retail Store for Customers." about.com. http://retail.about.com/od/storeoperations/a/store_recovery.htm

Wilburn, Gin. "Upside Down Christmas Tree Has Unique Design Benefits." 24 Nov. 2009. EzineArticles.com. http://ezinearticles.com/?Upside-Down-Christmas-Tree—Has-Unique-Design-Benefits&id=3322388

The Essential Skills: Customer Service Vocabulary Building Workbook is suitable for use in secondary-school business and life-skills programs, ESL programs, and any training geared towards workplace essential skills development. This workbook will help you to:

✓ Develop the vocabulary and vocational skills you need to become successful in the field of customer service
✓ Improve your reading and oral communication skills
✓ Enhance your thinking and problem-solving skills
✓ Boost your spelling and phonics skills

The Essential Skills: Customer Service Vocabulary Building Workbook contains twelve modules and three review sections. The workbook introduces 274 words related to customer service and has ninety-two exercises to help build work-specific skills and job-related vocabulary. The exercises include:

✓ Find the Meaning   ✓ The Right Word   ✓ Apply the Meaning
✓ Fill in the Blanks   ✓ Reading Comprehension   ✓ Study the Word
✓ Synonyms   ✓ Antonyms   ✓ Analogies
✓ Word Search   ✓ Crossword   ✓ Plurals

About the Author

Jennifer resides with her family in Waterloo, Ontario. She has an honours degree in Sociology and a general degree in Psychology from Wilfrid Laurier University. Jennifer also has T.E.S.L. certification from Conestoga College and is a Registered Rehabilitation Professional. Jennifer is the owner and operator of Pathways Educational Services, an adult learning centre in Kitchener, Ontario. The company was founded in 2000 and since then has helped many adult learners to achieve academic and vocational success. Pathways has developed a reputation within the community for creating effective learning resources and for providing excellent programs that help adult learners to achieve success.

Our areas of specialization include:

✓ Essential Skills for the Workplace
✓ English as a Second Language
✓ Academic Upgrading
✓ GED Preparation
✓ Customer Service
✓ Computer Training
✓ Job Search Training